THE A-Z OF ANGLESEY

The A-Z of Anglesey

Margaret Hughes

ISBN: 0-86381-955-9

Cover design: Sian Parri

Published in 2005
by Gwasg Carreg Gwalch, Llanrwst.

Acknowledgments

My thanks go to many for allowing me to encroach upon their time and being so willing to share their knowledge. In particular to:

- the staff of Llangefni, Menai Bridge and Holyhead libraries;
- the Gwynedd and Anglesey Record Offices;
- writers to the Anglesey Antiquarian Society's Transactions;
- John Cave of the Holyhead Maritime Museum;
- Miss L. Townshend, Environment Officer, Menter Môn;
- Frances Cattaran, Director of the North Wales Wildlife Trust;
- Alun M. Owen, Countryside Officer, Isle of Anglesey County Council;
- Mr J. Beardsley, Master, Anglesey Hunt;
- Alun Gruffydd and John Smith of Oriel Ynys Môn;
- Ed Pari-Jones and J.C. Davies for permission to use their photographs;
- and to Gwasg Carreg Gwalch, Llanrwst, for continued valued service.

Any errors in the script are the author's.

A Glossary of Welsh place-names

Anglesey (Isle of Anglesey)	Môn (Ynys Môn)
Beaumaris	Biwmares
Church Bay	Porth Swtan
Holy Island	Ynys Cybi
Holyhead	Caergybi
Menai Bridge	Porthaethwy
Menai Strait	Afon Menai
Newborough	Niwbwrch
North Stack	Ynys Arw
Point Lynas	Y Leinws
Puffin Island	Ynys Seiriol
Red Wharf Bay	Traeth Coch
South Stack	Ynys Lawd
Swellies	Pwll Ceris

Words frequently used in place-names:

big	mawr/fawr
bay	bae
hill	allt/bryn
mountain	mynydd
river	afon
brook	nant
chapel	capel
beach	traeth
cemetery	mynwent

Contents

A

Access in the 19th century – A revolution

To appreciate travelling on the Isle of Anglesey in the 19th century, one must remember times past.

Travelling over the island before 1826 was attempted only out of necessity. Access was difficult, roads were, for the most part, tracks and pathways. Before the 19th century began, comparatively few people came out of curiosity or as tourists – most travelled with the intention of reaching Holyhead to join a packet boat for Ireland.

Travellers from England made the hazardous journey along the northern coast of Wales or through the mountains to cross the Menai Strait by the Bangor or Porthaethwy ferry before striking one or other of the two post roads which converged at Ceint and then through Llangefni, Bodffordd, Llanynghenedl, Pontrhydbont (Four Mile Bridge) and on to the port at Holyhead. Many would travel light for the short sea crossing, having left their heavy baggage at Chester or Parkgate. These ports ran unpredictable ferry services to Ireland and were at the mercy of tides and weather. The luggage would be off-loaded at Dublin as and when the ship arrived.

The Menai ferry boats could transport horses as well as passengers. Even a coach, dismantled from its chassis, could be accommodated. The Abergwyngregyn-Beaumaris ferry passed over the Lavan sands which were treacherous at all times. Gradually this crossing lost popularity when travellers found the Bangor ferry to be shorter and safer.

The state of the roads over the island, if indeed they could be called roads, was atrocious, even after turnpiking which forced parishes to take some responsibility for the upkeep of their particular stretch of the highway. The way from Penmynydd to Llangefni was notorious for accidents. Today's Dragon Farm recalls the days when coachmen had to apply the 'drag' to the wheels if they were not to end in a sorry heap at the foot of the hill. No traveller across Anglesey in those days regarded the island as being flat.

In addition to passengers for Ireland, other frequent travellers were the post boys and mail coachmen. Towards the end of the 17th century the postal service to Holyhead became regular. Innkeepers at the more important stopping places were the country's first postmasters, being paid to stable horses for the use of the post boys and for hire. Beaumaris was one such Post Office until it was superseded by Bangor as that ferry crossing was preferred.

All this was to change from 1801 when the Act of Union with Ireland came into force. Suddenly the London to Holyhead route assumed extra importance, and it was realised that something had to be done about the state of the highway from London through northern Wales, the Anglesey stretch included.

Thomas Telford was commissioned to survey, report, and suggest ways of improving this important route which, it was expected, would see a great increase in traffic as a result of the Act.

Telford's report did not mince words:

The journey of the Mail coach across Anglesey is accessed in three hours ten minutes,' he wrote. 'I consider this rate of travelling to be quite unsafe on the present road. The steepness and length of the hills prevents the Mail from being driven fast up them, not faster than a very slow walk in some instances. The consequence is that the coachmen, in order to keep the time, drive at a most furious and dangerous pace down the whole of them, with little or no regard to the rate of inclination, the narrowness of the road or the numerous bends on it. They let their horses go at the top of a hill and take their chance of a coach finding its way in safety to the bottom. That it ever does so is a matter of mere accident as the drivers have never in such cases any power over it.

As well as the steep hilly stretches, Telford reminded the committee of the poor width of the road in some places – only twelve feet wide with many sharp turns and the sides unprotected. He was of the opinion that if the present line was to be preserved the whole road would need to be re-made, a costly business, and so he advocated a new line of road in its place.

This, too, would be costly. The Committee thought long and hard before agreeing with his suggestion. A new road was delineated to run west of the old post road, cutting across Anglesey along the more low-lying land from Porthaethwy, close to Llanfairpwll, Gaerwen, avoiding Llangefni, to Gwalchmai, Bryngwran, Caergeiliog and over a new embankment to the outskirts of Holyhead on Holy Island. As a result, the villages named would creep up to the new road, making new communities.

Most of Telford's road was completed and in use by 1822.

This was a purpose-built road, and not an old highway brought up to date. It was a road with a surface designed primarily to take Mail coaches with passengers and it would also stimulate private traffic. So the road surface was intended to be hard-wearing, to withstand weight and wheels and created with the most modern techniques known at the time. The Romans had worked on the principle

11

that the natural ground surface beneath the road should carry the brunt of the traffic weight, rather than the upper surface. This was the principle that Telford also adopted. He planned a substantial foundation with layers of metalling. Different types of land demanded different amounts of grounding, for the Holyhead road ran across both stony and boggy ground on its way across the island.

The base of Telford's road was laid with a nine-inch camber, higher at the crown than at the sides. The surface of paving was overlaid with five or six inches of broken stones of even size and covered with a thin coat of gravel to smooth the surface. This top surface needed constant maintenance. Telford allowed it to weather over the first winter while it compacted. In the spring the roadmen filled any potholes and re-surfaced where necessary. This was an on-going practice.

Gravel and stone were stored in small depots on the roadside, conveniently placed and, jutting out from the road. Some of these depots still remain along the length of the A5 today. They were a characteristic of the Holyhead road. It was ordered that they should be 'no more than a quarter of a mile apart so as to admit of moving the materials in barrows'. They had to be 'twelve yards long and the two dyke works each two yards and a half at the bottom', each to hold twenty-four cubic yards of stone. The depots were strongly built and paved with sandstone flags with an earth bank around the outside. Similar depots were interspersed wherever they were deemed necessary.

Five tollhouses were built and gates erected at Llanfairpwll, Nant, Gwalchmai, Caergeiliog and the Stanley Embankment. Travellers had to stop to pay for entry to the next section so the journey was not without its frustrations. Toll charges can still be seen on the upper wall of the Llanfairpwll tollhouse.

Increased road traffic demanded new roadside facilities.

The old post road traffic had been well serviced by the popular inn at Gwyndy, Ty'n Llan, sometimes referred to as Gwindy. Today only crumbling ivy-clad walls and chimneys remain of this once popular inn. With the opening of the new road a new half-way inn was built on Caeau Môn near Gwalchmai and named The Mona Inn. This is now a farmhouse. The enterprise was not to be successful for long as road traffic dwindled when the railway to Holyhead was completed.

At Holyhead there were several inns to cope with the demands of travellers embarking and disembarking at the port, the most famous being the 'Eagle and Child'. Situated at the south end of Market Street, this had been built about 1770 and was conveniently placed alongside the first quay used by sailing packets. King George IV visited on his way to Ireland in 1821. When the Railway Hotel was built at the station entrance in 1880 the 'Eagle and Child' lost its importance and was eventually converted into the houses now known as Victoria Terrace.

The new Holyhead road was at its busiest during the late 1820s and 1830s, especially after Thomas Telford had built his suspension bridge over the Menai Strait and thus dispelling the hazard of the ferry crossing to Anglesey.

Spanning the Menai Strait with a road bridge taxed the ingenuity of several engineers for some years. Telford initially presented designs for two cast iron bridges but the Admiralty turned these and an earlier design by John Rennie down stipulating that it was necessary for large vessels to pass below the bridge with masts erect. In 1818 Telford submitted his final design which was accepted. Work began immediately. During its construction the bridge was a source of interest to many onlookers who followed its progress until it was opened to traffic. The last chain was suspended in July 1825 and the occasion marked by a military band which marched along a temporary platform to the centre to play the National Anthem while a steamship sailed below to re-open the channel to shipping.

Telford himself was among the first travellers to cross the completed bridge, leading a queue of coaches and carriages, riders on horseback and pedestrians. At last, the way was clear from mainland Wales to Holyhead, the journey time cut by hours and made far more comfortable than hitherto.

But soon there was yet another route for travellers to Anglesey in the offing. Everywhere in Britain coach travel was being superseded by train journeys. Again with improvement of access to the Irish ferries in mind, plans were being laid to cross the Menai Strait by train and to take the railway to Holyhead.

Two possible routes were discussed, one to take goods and passengers to Porthdinllaen on the Llŷn peninsula and develop it as a port for Ireland, and the other to Holyhead. The Holyhead point of embarkation was preferred. In 1845 Robert Stephenson was appointed engineer-in-chief to the Chester and Holyhead Railway with the challenging task of crossing the Menai Strait. He devised a huge tubular bridge of riveted plates. The work was carried out in an area on the waterside and this, too, drew much public attention and speculation. The day the giant tubes were lifted into position on the massive stone columns drew the crowds in their hundreds.

In March 1850 the first train, carrying seven hundred passengers and forty-five wagons of coal reached Anglesey. Stephenson's Britannia Bridge was to remain the rail link between Caernarfonshire and Anglesey until the 1970s when a chance fire swept through the tubes, buckling them severely, and Anglesey lost its rail link with the mainland until the bridge was rebuilt with the addition of an overhead roadway, as we see it today.

The two bridges were to bring a new type of traveller to Anglesey – the holidaymaker and the tourist who came to explore its delights.

B

Britannia took her toll

It was quiet down on the shore of the Menai Strait, below St Mary's churchyard in Llanfairpwll. A receding tide had left shingle strewn with the detritus of modern living – a plastic bag, a torn carton, a bottle – caught between the fronds of seaweed. The water lapped a farewell around the plinth of the Nelson statue with a soft swooshing sound. A lone gull mewed as it flew overhead, to disappear under the arch of the Britannia Bridge.

The opposite shore was lush with growth, trees down to the water's edge hiding the one remaining section of box girder from the original rail bridge, placed there as a reminder of what was once one of the engineering wonders of Britain.

The seat in the churchyard was occupied by a young man looking through binoculars across the water towards Plas Newydd and Yr Eifl beyond. I had to pass in front of him to regain the path. He lowered his binoculars and gave a friendly nod.

'Beautiful morning!' he greeted me with a strong Midlands accent. 'This is a peaceful spot. Never been here before. What's the story behind the statue down there on the shore, d'you know?'

That was an invitation to converse. He made room for me on the seat and I introduced him to Admiral Clarence Paget, one time Admiral of the Mediterranean fleet and son of the first Marquess of Anglesey, and his intention to erect a statue as a landmark for the many ships which, in his day, sailed through the Menai Strait. Nelson was Paget's hero.

My young friend's curiosity knew no bounds. He wanted to know about the Britannia Bridge, its builder Robert Stephenson; how the massive box girders were lifted into place, and 'who made the four lions guarding the entrances?'

I guided his attention to the boundary wall of the churchyard.

'I thought that was a war memorial,' he commented, indicating the squat stone column standing high above the wall.

We walked up closer and he read the inscription, commemorating those who had lost their lives as Stephenson's bridge was being built. Sixteen workmen who toiled in constant danger died as a result of injuries sustained while they worked in the days when Health & Safety regulations were but a pipe dream. These men had their own code. It was every man for himself, and the possibility of accident through carelessness was a constant menace.

When one remembers how many men were involved in the massive project, the number of fatalities was relatively small. There were seven hundred masons, eight hundred men worked on the box girders, seven hundred more floated the completed tubes out to mid stream and thirty-six raised them to their final positions.

Three large workshops were built on wooden platforms on the water side where forges and specially designed machinery cut and punched the iron plates. During the years 1846-50, the once quiet banks of the Menai Strait were transformed into an industrial site, with a shanty village rising up almost overnight to house the workers, many of whom had come over from Yorkshire to labour on the prestigious project. The Strait became a hive of activity. Stone, iron, and other materials were unloaded at five wharves created for the purpose. Six steam engines helped to raise stone for the towers (sandstone from Runcorn and Anglesey marble from Penmon) and powered the workshop machinery.

The temporary wooden huts housed families who were provided with a shop, a school, a doctor and a clergyman.

It was a dangerous place for adventurous children. One wonders what happened to Emma Greave of Wakefield, the five year old child whose death is commemorated on the memorial. Did she drown? Or did she die from disease? We are not told. Living conditions in the village would leave much to be desired, even by poor working-class standards, with little or no sanitary provision. Typhus was a constant threat and just as likely to attack a white-collar worker as a labourer. Young, twenty-seven year old accountant William Brook of Dewsbury fell ill and died of the dreaded disease. The memorial praises his attributes.

Children as young as nine or ten worked as riveters' assistants, being nimble enough to reach the most awkward positions. Rivets would be red hot when thrown, to be caught expertly and rammed home while still malleable. A slip could cause a tragedy.

Plating and lifting the gigantic box girders were not without problems. Fatalities occurred when large presses occasionally failed to lift, allowing the girders to slip. This accident accounted for some of the deaths noted on the memorial.

The plan to provide a huge statue of Britannia for the top of one of the towers had to be abandoned due to lack of funds but four stone lions, designed and fashioned by sculptor John Thomas, were placed at the entrances to the tubes. John Thomas was a Gloucestershire orphan who went to work for his architect brother in Birmingham and was eventually chosen by Sir Charles Barry to be responsible for the statues on the north and south fronts of the House of Commons, the panels bearing the arms of the kings and queens of England from William the Conqueror to Queen Victoria. He also designed and made the statues and bosses for the Victoria Tower and the bosses in St Stephens Hall. Each Britannia Bridge lion is twenty-five feet long and weighs eighty tons. Lifting them into position, two at each end of the bridge, was a recipe for disaster.

My young friend gazed contemplatively at the bridge.

'So what happened to those iron tubes?' he asked. I realised that he could be too young to remember. In 1970 the bridge was set alight by accident, when teenagers threw flaming paper into the rafters to disturb roosting bats. The rafters had been covered with tarred canvas, so they were highly combustible. A strong wind fanned the flames and in no time the whole bridge was on fire, from end to end. As a result the girders broke apart at the side joints over the piers as they cooled, and the main tubes sagged over two feet at midspan.

Steel arches have replaced the tubes, and a roadway has been built above the rail track. This was another marathon exercise, but this time with the advantage of modern technology.

He turned to look at the memorial once more, and read the names of the two men who lost their lives during this re-building.

'So Britannia took her toll again,' he commented wryly, as we walked up the path towards the churchyard gate.

C

Country jottings

The Anglesey Record Office in Llangefni stores many treasures which increase our knowledge of how life was lived on the island generations ago.

One of the most colourful – and, indeed, the most eccentric – is a somewhat scrappy diary written in the 1870s by two sisters, Mary and Ann Jones, who farmed at Tŷ Hen, Coedana. Welsh was obviously their first language, but for some reason they wrote their diary in a perplexing mixture of Welsh and English. They knew little of comparative idioms and their English phraseology was often a direct translation from the Welsh. Their spelling was careless, their handwriting frequently difficult to read, and yet these roughly written diary entries paint a vivid picture of a hard life on the land.

Mary and Ann Jones kept a maid, Catherine. The sisters were regular chapelgoers and observed the tradition of family prayers when they and their workers would meet in the farm kitchen before a day's work.

The first diary entry reads:

This book written to Remember for Mary Jones and Ann Jones, Tŷ Hen. The way with Grefydd [Religion] and to Farm.

The readings for April 1874 were listed, one biblical

reading for each day of the month.

The sisters were Calvinistic Methodists. They refer to attending meetings of the 'Sasiwn', or business meetings, and the services connected with them when they would listen to preachers of note. Diary entries for the days when these were held consist of notes on the sermons and the texts – all these in between mention of hoeing turnips and attending to the sheep and cattle.

> Mary Jones and Ann Jones go to everything in chapel pob yn ail [alternately], Sunday night both two.

Their duties on the farm were varied.

> May 2, Saturday: Done Rowli cornfield. To plant three rows of Tadw [potatoes] at 64 rows before harrowing and 28 after harrowing. This three rows is next to Lôn bach [the little lane].

> May 4, Monday: Begin manage sweets [swedes] and turnips land one side of garden after priddo [earthing] Tadw [potatoes]. Dyddyfnu [weaned] three lambs, the sheep cloff [lame] nine weeks of age. Morning next day Mary Jones to give milk to the little lambs. And Ann Jones to go to milk the sheep.

The following Saturday they took ' . . . six and a half Quarter of oats at Amlwch,' and returned with 'five hundred of guano'. Guano was regularly delivered by sea to Amlwch, for farmers to fertilise their land.

The sisters lived in a close community where respect was shown to the dead and to the bereaved families. On Sunday May 10: ' . . . Ann Jones in wylnos [a wake] for John Owen, Ynys Coed'. The following day ' . . . Mary Jones yn cynebrwn John Owen yn Llandyfrydog' [Mary Jones at John

Owen's funeral at Llandyfrydog].

The maid, Catherine, had been courting and was to be married that month. But Ann wrote:

Saturday night, 23: Was John Thomas [the bridegroom] with Catherine in bed, and priodi [to be married] Monday.

The maid confessed:

Catherine said to John Thomas been in the House to love nine time and two time down in priws [brewhouse], one time in Crowa (?), one week every night before go off from Gwredog.

Then, a final comment: 'Mary Jones to hear'. The errant couple were married on Whit Monday, but the event took second place in the diary to: 'Open sweets [swedes] rows'.

Old remedies were popular. Ann would appear to have been the healthier of the two sisters, but she did note one occasion when she herself needed assistance from her sister:

11th June, 1874: Gofidiau oedd yn fy ysgwydd wedi darfod trwy i Mary Jones ei chwipio â Dalen Poethion, a chwysu Dail Adar y Wrach a'i roddi ar yr ysgwydd. Yr oedd y Gofidion mor fawr fel y bum nos saboth heb cysgu. [The trouble in my shoulder ended after Mary Jones whipped it with nettles, and put a poultice of burdock leaves on the shoulder. The trouble was so bad I spent a sleepless night on Sunday.]

But by 3rd August she was much improved, and went out with her gun on a local shoot. Ann's aim, however, was not all it should have been:

. . . First ergid I did give saethais clomen Miss Prichard, Plas Medd. Roddais Testament value four shillings and six pence to her because that. [With my first attempt I shot the pigeon belonging to Miss Prichard, Plas Medd . . . Gave her a Testament valued at four shillings and sixpence because of that.]

Not all was hard graft, however. There are references to one sister, it is not clear which, being 'with Côr Mawr in Town Hall, Llangefni' [with the big choir at the Town Hall, Llangefni], and the following week 'with Côr Mawr to Caernarfon'.

As farmers, they had to be prepared for every eventuality with calving, lambing and taking care of their stock:

July 1st: I to rise one clock this to wait the sow to bring little pigs. It came 14.

Mary found farming hard work, as Ann records when she wrote: 'trawyd she yn sal after work too much' [she was taken ill after working to hard].

In January 1875 Mary was ill again:

I buy Potel of fisig by William Thomas Drigist for ten Penny. But at end of week she is little better . . . She have not been in the chapel this week.

In between the chores of digging potatoes, cutting hay, collecting stones, milking, clearing bracken and going to market the sisters had the occasional social contact to enjoy. On Sunday, 30 August, 1874, Ann was invited to Ann Evans presumably of a neighbouring farm or house, to take tea:

Sent Ann Evans want me to go there for Tê afternoon three o'clock I went there. I had Bara prith, Teisen and full between two cristin of good thing. [Ann Evans invited me for afternoon tea. I went there at three o'clock . . . I had currant bread, cake and a good, well-filled sandwich.]

Another time she lists some hints on how to behave at afternoon tea:

From Misses Prichard . . . to drink tea – cup into left hand, bread into right hand. Begin tywallt part of cup to sawsar and to give cup on hambwr, when cup to cold at end, drink from cup and give it sawser. Bread in the right hand some time cut tamad with hand to mouth and another time mouth cut tamad.

[From Misses Prichard . . . to drink tea – cup into left hand, bread into right hand. Begin pouring part of cup into saucer and put cup on tray. When cup cold, drink from cup and put it on the saucer. Bread in the right hand and break off a piece with the hand to the mouth, and another time bite the piece of bread.]

There is a note at the end of the diary, written in another hand after the sisters' death, which gives personal details. Mary was born in 1807 and died in 1890. Ann's dates are quoted as 1809-1896.

Their deaths are recorded in sentimental fashion:

Caeodd Mary Jones ei llygaid 9 Medi 1890. Ann Jones, 10 Gorffennaf, yn 87 mlwydd oed. [Mary Jones closed her eyes 9 September 1890. Ann Jones 10 July, 87 years of age.]

D

Digging – before it's too late

Today a vast amount of surveying and decision-making goes on before a new road becomes a reality. Where the terrain is likely to contain sites of archaeological importance the work becomes all the more complicated.

When Thomas Telford laid his Holyhead road across the island in the early years of the 19th century, little regard was given to such historical research. Two hundred years later it is a very different story.

This initial assessment for what we now call the A55 dual carriageway expressway began in 1993 when the proposed route was examined and considered in relation to the known archaeological sites. Aerial photographs were taken. This was to be the third attempt to cross the island.

The first route was the age-old, meandering route, from Beaumaris and Porthaethwy through Ceint, Llangefni, Bodffordd, Llanynghenedl and Pont Rhydbont. It was used by travellers to reach the port at Holyhead, and by drovers and farmers taking their cattle and sheep to the Menai Strait crossings to the mainland, the English towns and cities, and Welsh markets. As coach travel increased the sharp corners and steep hills caused accidents. Telford's Holyhead Road avoided difficult contours. Now indicated by brown signs baring a coach and horses logo, the A5 as it is known cut corners, traversed lower ground and made the journey faster and more comfortable.

By the end of the 20th century closer links between Ireland and Europe and consequently heavier traffic demanded yet another route. So Euro Route 22 was born – the A55. It was to be eight years before the road was finally completed and opened to traffic.

Once the line of the new road was determined, a field evaluation was made, a geophysical survey carried out, and trial excavations began. These brought to light a number of rich sites covering several periods – enough interest to make the archaeologists happy and the road developers fear that deadlines would not be met. In the end all was well. The archaeologists had widened their knowledge through a number of finds, the contractors finished the job, and 21st century travellers to and from Ireland and those coming to Anglesey to visit the beaches and local attractions are content with the hassle-free journey along a well metalled road.

A number of sites were excavated, notably at Capel Eithin, Gaerwen; Cefn Cwmwd, and Melin y Plas, Cefndu.

The finds varied. There were faience beads of around 1500 BC made from a core of sand and crushed quartz coated with copper glaze which, when new, would have been a pretty blue-green.

A shale fastener was found, possibly burnt at cremation about the same era. There were flint tools, hammer stones, Bronze Age urns, stone mortars, Roman mixing bowls and brooches, shards of Roman and Samian pottery, whet-stones and spindle whorls, all pointing to activity on the island many centuries ago.

At Cefn Cwmwd the settlement continued after the Romans left. The population was evidently in touch with international trading routes as a shard from a platter made in south-west France and rarely found in Britain, came to light.

Another interesting discovery was two small pieces of

Cheshire bisquetage from ceramic vessels used to dry salt in Cheshire, then brought to Wales, the only pottery used on Anglesey during the period c.500 BC to AD 50.

Three years after the A55 expressway was opened to traffic an exhibition of the artefacts, aerial and other photographs and paintings, and a comprehensive description of the detailed preparatory work which had taken place was staged at Oriel Ynys Môn. This created great interest. Had it not been for all the preparatory work these artefacts might never have been discovered.

What other treasures lie, still to be unearthed, beneath Anglesey soil?

E

Ecclesiastical architects at work in Anglesey

Today, when churches and chapels are closing for want of support, it is difficult to imagine the surge of religious fervour during the 19th century, which brought about the restoration of many Anglesey church buildings and the erection of scores of chapels for the Nonconformists.

But for this enthusiasm, many ancient churches would be in ruins. Twenty-seven of the old churches on Anglesey were rebuilt during the reign of Queen Victoria. Most of the remainder were restored or refitted, while eleven new ones were built, some on different sites.

Professor M.L. Clark made a survey in 1952 and recorded his findings for the Transactions of the Anglesey Antiquarian Society. They make interesting reading.

He commented, as have many architects since, that the work done then was of little architectural value. Money could have been at the root of this, as parishes had little to spare.

Changing styles in church architecture prompted some of the work, especially when it became fashionable to add a tower (as at Llandegfan and Llangeinwen). A new church was built at Brynsiencyn to replace the ancient Llanidan parish church down by the Menai Strait, and the same happened at Llanffinan on the Pentreberw to Ceint road. The old Llanffinan church, now ruined, stands in a clump of vegetation in a field on the other side of the road.

In one or two places the population of a parish had grown to such an extent that a new building was necessary. St Elbod's church in the centre of Amlwch is a case in point. It was built in 1800 to meet the spiritual needs of a growing population working in the Mynydd Parys copper industry.

For their restoration, existing churches sometimes took on the preferences of their patrons. One has only to remember the Muslim blue tiles of the décor at Llanbadrig, which reflected the Mahommedan beliefs of the then Lord Stanley, although he was also a keen supporter of the Church in Wales.

But for the financial support of individuals and the gentry, many of the restoration projects would never have taken place.

Local architects working from their Bangor offices designed many of the alterations to Anglesey churches. Men like John Hall and Henry Kennedy. Others from outside Wales were commissioned, too, when finances allowed – Weightman and Hadfield of Sheffield restored Penmon and designed St Seiriol's church, Holyhead, now demolished, and Sir Gilbert Scott, revered by the profession in his day, restored St Cybi's church in Holyhead.

An interesting feature of Anglesey church architecture of the 19th century is the number of instances when the clergy themselves were the architects. The buildings at Heneglwys and Trewalchmai were re-built on the old plan, the Rev. J. Wynne Jones acting as architect. The Rev. Peter Jones built Llanddona church to his own design. Llanfair-yng-Nghornwy church was restored under the direction of the Rev. James Williams.

Kennedy churches on Anglesey include Llandysilio, the church on the steep rise opposite the Anglesey Arms hotel in Menai Bridge; Llannerch-y-medd, Llanfaelog, Llanfair Mathafarn Eithaf, Llanfair-yn-neubwll, Llanfihangel

Esgeifiog, Llanfwrog, Llangoed, Llangristiolus, and several more.

The early chapels were usually plain and box-like consisting of merely four walls and a door. They were designed by the ministers who served their early congregations until the number of adherents increased as nonconformity became the popular form of worship on Anglesey.

Larger premises were needed, so architects were commissioned from 1850. The old, square plan gave way to a more sophisticated layout. By 1851 nonconformity was more popular here than was the established church, and the new chapels reflected this in their size and style.

Several architects began to specialise in designing chapels. Richard Davies, a carpenter's son, with his office in Bangor, designed many chapels over northern Wales between 1867 and 1905. These were plain buildings, but nevertheless had touches of originality, as at Capel Mawr, Amlwch, whose 'Sêt Fawr' (the long, enclosed seat below the pulpit occupied by the chapel elders) had two central panels which could be opened to allow a wedding to take place.

Richard Griffith Thomas was consultant to the Baron Hill estate of the Williams Bulkeley family outside Beaumaris, but he also took commissions for eight chapels. He lived in Menai Bridge where his English Presbyterian chapel was built with money from the wealthy Treborth family, in the style of a church. All very far removed from the folksy-style boxes of half a century earlier.

He also designed the Victoria Hotel next to the chapel – similarities in style are obvious. Richard Griffith Thomas died in 1909 from injuries sustained after falling from the roof of the hotel.

Joseph Owen, another local architect, lived on Hill Street, Menai Bridge. He designed three chapels in Amlwch.

The discerning visitor walking around Anglesey towns and villages today will notice buildings which were obviously chapels at one time, but have now been converted for other uses, usually apartments or restaurants. Others still retain their dignified appearance, reminders of the days when Sunday worshippers filled their pews, and of the men who designed them.

F

Four philanthropists

Every age has produced its philanthropists, men who have made their way in the world and ploughed back a generous proportion of their gains for the good of their fellow men in their own communities.

Anglesey can claim at least four who had ties with the island and were liberal with their gifts.

The large modern comprehensive school building on the hill above Menai Bridge carries the name of David Hughes, a name to be reckoned with in Anglesey since the 17th century.

It is believed that David Hughes may have been born at Llantrisant around 1536. Although little is known of his early years, he was appointed steward of the manor of Woodrising in Norfolk at some stage, and there became an important person. Although David Hughes spent many years away from his native Anglesey, he looked upon the island with affection. He founded the 'Free Grammar School' in Beaumaris in 1602, and also made provision for almshouses where the poor could be housed and maintained. By this time he was sufficiently wealthy to have bought land in Anglesey. In his will he endowed the school with the income from this land. He stipulated that any income left after paying the masters and the upkeep of the school building should be used for two purposes – to provide scholarships for worthy pupils to extend their education at Oxford or Cambridge and to build almshouses for eight poor people who were to receive 'six shillings and six yards of cloth on St Thomas's Day'. The income he bequeathed increased along with the value of the land.

David Hughes's intention was to provide education for local children, but the ensuing years saw great changes. The reputation of Beaumaris Free Grammar School attracted pupils from farther afield. Fees were then charged, which restricted the education to those who could afford to pay.

By 1850 it had become a boarding school for children of the wealthier families. By 1867 there were only nine day pupils and only seven of those were local children. But gradually the character of the school changed again; the curriculum was broadened, and more Anglesey children were accepted at lower fees.

The original school building which still stands near the castle moat in Beaumaris is now used as the town's community centre. With the revolution in education during the 20th century the large new comprehensive school in Menai Bridge absorbed the pupils from Beaumaris as the catchment area extended.

It is good to see that David Hughes's philanthropic gesture of 1602 to provide education for Anglesey children is remembered to this day by the adoption of his name for the Menai Bridge school.

Over two hundred years later, another David Hughes was to leave his mark on the north of the island. He was a carpenter from Cemaes who, like many of his contemporaries, left Anglesey to work in the house-building boom in the rapidly expanding port of Liverpool.

David Hughes saw his opportunities and grasped them. He set up his own business as a builder and made a fortune. Anglesey was always close to his heart. He built himself a home at Cemaes, where the Wylfa Magnox Power Station now stands and, in 1898, financed and built the Village Hall at Cemaes at a cost of £2,500. Centrally placed on the High Street, its fifty-feet high clock tower remains a focal point, and over a century on, the Hall is still used regularly by local societies for meeting and social gatherings.

The name Stanley is often seen in Holyhead. The family home was at Penrhos, on the outskirts of the town. William Owen Stanley was born in Cheshire in 1802, one of twin sons of the first Lord Stanley of Alderley. He married Ellin, daughter of Sir John Williams of Bodelwyddan, and the couple made their home at Penrhos.

For thirty-four years William Owen Stanley served as Member of Parliament for Anglesey, Beaumaris, and Chester. He was Lord Lieutenant of Anglesey and a Justice of the Peace. He is remembered for his antiquarian interests – he excavated widely on Holy Island in 1862 and 1868 – and for his generosity to the people and town of Holyhead.

When the mail coach service was established he converted an old house into an inn for travellers at the stage terminus on the shore of the tidal harbour, which he named 'Eagle & Child' after the family crest.

In 1866 the family established the Penrhos Almshouses Trust at twelve cottages in the Kingsland area. William Owen Stanley built the covered market, a vast improvement on the previous open air facility. In 1872 he donated over £4,500 towards the provision of the Stanley Hospital on Salt Island, and the Stanley Sailors' Home. In 1877 he contributed a large sum towards the restoration of St Cybi's church. He was also responsible for providing a water supply for the town.

When William Owen Stanley died his funeral was an event to be remembered for many years by the inhabitants of Holyhead who had much reason to be grateful to 'the grand old political chieftain and one of the kindest and most considerate of landlords', as one newspaper reporter described him.

There is always an added frisson of interest about a philanthropist whose beginnings were lowly.

This might be said of John Prichard-Jones who came of farming stock and whose parents lived in a small cottage at Newborough during the middle of the 19th century. On leaving school at fourteen John was sent to Caernarfon where he was apprenticed to a draper. At that time Caernarfon was something of a metropolis, a centre of trade, a busy port, and the nearest town of any size to the south-western coast of Anglesey. It was, in those days, approached by ferry from Y Foel.

After completing his apprenticeship, the young draper had his sights on advancement, and left Wales to work in England, eventually joining the staff of Dickens' Regent Street shop in London in 1874. Here he rose quickly to positions of responsibility, and eventually became a director and chairman of the company, to which he added his own name – Dickens & Jones.

During this time John never forgot his roots. His regard for Wales strengthened with the years. He held many public offices, among them Sheriff of Anglesey in 1905, treasurer of the National Museum, a member of the Council of North Wales University College at Bangor and Vice President of the Council. He gave his name to the University's large assembly hall. He had a country home at Dwyran, close to Newborough.

John Prichard-Jones was knighted for his public service.

Thanks to his generosity, Newborough has a fine community centre and a group of almshouses. The substantial building he financed a little over one hundred years ago still plays an important role in village life. It contains a library, a public hall, coffee room, reading room, and on two sides of the pleasant front courtyard are the almshouses, spruce and attractive still.

Today the Prichard-Jones charity is run by a Trust. The

buildings are all Grade II* listed, and well cared for. The aims of the late Sir John Prichard-Jones are still uppermost in the minds of the residents of Newborough.

These are four of Anglesey's more well known philanthropists. There have been others whose impact had been felt on small local communities, most perhaps during the 19th and early 20th centuries which have been called 'the age of philanthropy'.

G

Gardeners' delight

Today's trend towards opening private gardens to the public in aid of charity has resulted in a surge of interest and a quest for knowledge of their history.

Anglesey has several such gardens, some accessible on certain days (The National Gardens Scheme Yellow Book lists them), others remaining private as personal horticultural jewels. And some of Anglesey's gardens of the past are merely memories now, eradicated or changed out of all recognition with time and development, but recalled on written record.

William Bulkeley, the 18th century diarist whose home was at Brynddu, Llanfechell, was the proud owner of a walled garden – an undoubted bonus on an island where strong winds are the norm and would otherwise play havoc with planting. William had been widowed early. He was a country squire who rarely left Anglesey, but his diary does record a visit to Dublin where he bought trees – English elm, apples, currant bushes, and dwarf box for edging the beds in his walled garden. He was not particularly interested in flowers, although there is a brief mention of 'a spring garden', but the emphasis is on trees, vegetables and herbs.

The amount of pleasure William Bulkeley derived from working in his garden is echoed in the number of references he makes in his diary. He grew potatoes, kidney beans, cabbage, cauliflowers, onions and asparagus, as well as many herbs. He sowed cowslip seed, not for the visual beauty of the flowers, but to harvest them to make cowslip wine. He grafted plums, apples and cherries. Many of the trees standing around the old house today are there thanks to William Bulkeley's diligence.

In February 1750 he wrote: 'I finished planting all the Trees I intend to plant this year, having planted . . . young Oak about two feet high, some few walnut Trees and Black Cherries. I likewise planted a few Apple Trees . . . & 2 Fig Trees besides the eight large Sycamore Trees that I mentioned before . . . & Some few Aspen Trees and Alders.' In all, he planted 454 trees during his lifetime.

He made a hot bed to 'transplant Mellons and Cucumber into it'.

In 1751 William went to Llanlleiana: 'simpling', to gather herbs for his garden, and in 1760 was accompanied by another Anglesey gardener, the botanist and herbalist William Morris, who gardened at Holyhead.

William Morris's garden has long disappeared beneath bricks and mortar and tarmac, but his copious correspondence with his brothers living elsewhere paints a word picture of his knowledge and enthusiasm for the craft.

William Morris's first garden was a joint effort with his friend, the Rev. Thomas Ellis, and was a small flourishing plot. This was not enough, and he prepared what he termed 'a new pleasure garden' which, over the years, he extended from the rocky site on which his house was built above the town down to the Roman wall surrounding St Cybi's church. This was a triangular garden. By 1758 he had 'planted chiefly with flowering shrubs and serpentine walks'. His letters describe the garden in detail. He added, in Welsh: 'ni bu ddyn yn fyttach na myfi, cynnyg codi perllan ar graig y môr'. [There never was a more foolish man than I, attempting to raise an orchard on a rock above the sea.] But he knew the value of shelter made of quick-growing hedging, to break the wind, which allowed him then to nurture plants which would otherwise have been impossible to grow.

William Morris collected seed and plants wherever he could – his post as customs officer at the port introduced him to ships' captains who would bring him seed from overseas. His brother Richard was cajoled into sending 'samples' from his friends' gardens in London. He also begged from relatives working on country estates in England.

William Morris is famous as a botanist. His life-long interest could have stemmed from his mother, who was no mean herbalist herself. He searched for local plants, and listed them carefully so today we are aware of what grew in Anglesey in the 18th century, and where they could be found. Hugh Davies, in his *Welsh Botanology*, pays warm tribute to William Morris's extensive knowledge.

Like his friend William Bulkeley, Morris never found gardening a chore, but a pure delight.

No mention of Anglesey gardens of the past would be complete without a tribute to Elizabeth Morgan who gardened at Henblas, Llangristiolus. She came to Anglesey in 1734 from Herefordshire when she married Henry Morgan.

Elizabeth's garden diary, now safe in the Henblas Mss. begins in 1754 but there may have been an earlier volume. She obviously believed that an estate garden should be the province of the lady of the family, and her diary shows how well she carried out her assumed responsibility. She writes of 'the old garden' and 'the new garden' which suggests she had her own ideas and made sure they were carried out.

Elizabeth Morgan loved flowers. In her spring garden she grew single and double snowdrops, double primroses and polyanthus: ' . . . finished planting the Well walk and planted Thirteen Rings of Polyanthus on the border of the

"New Walk"'. One autumn she planted 285 tulip bulbs, and 353 hyacinths. She sowed annuals in season and planted roses, carnation slips and countless auriculas. Her garden must have been a riot of colour all the year round.

Henblas had not only a flower garden, but a rich vegetable plot as well. Elizabeth knew her housewifely responsibilities and her kitchen garden was equally well stocked with fruit, vegetables and herbs for all culinary and medicinal purposes. Like William Bulkeley, she bought her fruit trees in Dublin.

Elizabeth Morgan died in 1773, having kept her gardening diary for the best part of her life. Latterly she had to admit ' . . . at this time I had the Rheumatism in my left hand and could scarce put roots in the ground'.

The late 1700s saw much activity at Plas Newydd, Llanedwen, home of the Earl of Uxbridge. To coincide with the re-designing of the house it was decided to re-plan and plant the garden and park. Garden designer Humphrey Repton was commissioned to prepare plans which he duly did, submitting them in one of his now famous *Red Books*, which can be seen today at the house. Not all of his ideas were adopted, but 'Plantations ought to be encouraged to screen a bleak country and shelter the grounds from violent winds' was acknowledged to be wise.

Plas Newydd gardens today are the responsibility of the National Trust with the present Marquess of Anglesey taking a keen personal interest.

The grounds at Plas Newydd offer something to every gardener. The view from the house across the Menai Strait towards the mountains has altered little from the time when Humphrey Repton visited to make his assessment of the possibilities, apart from the development of Y Felinheli to the south-west, and the Britannia bridge to the east, but the woods and fields of the Faenol estate opposite have arrested any further development there.

The first Marquess of Anglesey (he of Waterloo fame) extended Repton's ideas, as did subsequent holders of the title. Early in the 20th century the 6th Marquess developed the woodland further, and today the glorious spring colour in the garden to the south-west, known as 'The West Indies', attracts visitors from all over the world. This is a garden of grand design, where big is beautiful. Azaleas, camellias, Japanese Maple, magnolias and other flowering shrubs compete with each other to grand effect.

Sixty years ago the site was very different, since this part of the garden was abandoned during wartime. Since then, immense effort and additional planting have worked wonders.

Plas Newydd is famous for its rhododendrons. In the spring, gardeners with a special interest in the species arrive from all parts of the world to visit and admire. The ground to the north-east of the house along the Strait, was first planted in the 1930s. This, too, was left to nature during the Second World War but cleared of invasive growth by the present Marquess in the years following. His marriage was marked by the late Lord Aberconwy with the gift of a great number of thinnings from Bodnant in the Conwy valley. Lord Aberconwy provided the labour to transplant them in their new home, where they have burgeoned to form the famous Plas Newydd Rhododendron Garden of today.

There are quiet corners at Plas Newydd, too. On the site of a conservatory north of the house, which has an elevated view across the water, an Italianate Garden gives welcome peace and quiet. Water splashes lazily from an arbour into a pool. There is a raised terrace flanked by large urns. The wide borders are full of perennial colour.

Like all successful gardens Plas Newydd has new features each year. The latest addition is a semicircular bed of low-growing late-flowering azaleas, planted in memory of one of the National Trust volunteers who served in the house as a steward for a number of years. They bring an eye-catching glimpse of bright colour under the trees in the upper part of 'The West Indies' at a time when earlier colour is fading.

Addison once wrote: 'I look upon the Pleasure which we took in a Garden as one of the Most Innocent Delights in human Life' – a sentiment which has been and still is reflected over the centuries in many Anglesey gardens.

H

Holyhead characters

Every town has its characters, some born locally and others being incomers who have made their mark.

Robert Roberts, born in Holyhead in 1777, was one such. He was the son of a publisher who printed the first Welsh Holyhead Almanac in 1741. Robert spent some time in London after being educated locally but returned to Holyhead at the age of 18 when his father died. He came home to carry on the printing business which his father had built up successfully and of which publishing the almanac was part. This appeared, without a break, for forty-four years.

Robert was a man of many interests. He opened a school where the curriculum was wide – arithmetic, reading and writing, book keeping, science, Latin and English grammar, geometry, and – suitable for the boys of Holyhead – navigation. He was a keen geographer and published maps in Welsh, probably the first cartographer to do so. He installed a telescope in the upper storey of his home with two purposes – to scan the night sky, and to pick up semaphore signals from ships afloat, for the Irish packet service. He was organist at St Cybi's church, being exceptionally knowledgeable about church music. He owned property in the town, was interested in agriculture, and was estate manager to the Penrhos estate for a time. All this activity was packed into a relatively short life of fifty-eight years.

Arriving in Holyhead during this period also, John McGregor Skinner was to have thirty years' association with the town. He was born in America about 1760, where his father was King's Attorney General for New Jersey. His early years were spent at sea where he lost an arm and an eye during the American War of Independence.

In 1799 Skinner changed tack, joined the Postal Service, and came to Holyhead to take charge of a packet boat on the Holyhead to Dublin service. Never one to mince words, he made his opinions about the management of the Postal Service known in no uncertain terms. The ships were poorly built, he complained, the fares too high and passenger accommodation left much to be desired. Holyhead was losing valuable trade because of these shortcomings.

In 1832 John McGregor Skinner was returning from Dublin in a packet boat when a high sea struck and broke into the bulwark where he was standing. He was swept into the water and it was not until some time later that his body came ashore a few miles from Holyhead.

The town mourned a popular citizen. The monument to him, erected by a group of friends, stands appropriately on the hill at Morawelon above the port, looking down on to the harbour where he spent so much of his time. The inscription reads: 'he was a man distinguished for his zeal, intrepidity and fidelity, his disinterested kindness and unbounded charity'. The Holyhead Maritime Museum has a painting of his house and one or two of his personal possessions.

William Owen Stanley of Penrhos who made his mark on the town of Holyhead, has already been noted as one of Anglesey's 'Four philanthropists'.

The turn of the century found another arrival who was to become one of its best known townspeople over a number of years.

He was William Bradwen Jones, in whose memory a

plaque was unveiled in the market place following his death in 1970.

Bradwen Jones was born in Caernarfon in 1892. His early years were spent as an employee of the Glynllifon estate. He came from a musical family, was a choirboy in Caernarfon and had piano and organ lessons. While working at Glynllifon he was allowed to play the organ in the house on occasions, and the family allowed him time off work to cycle to Bangor to take organ lessons at Bangor Cathedral.

He then moved to the Wynn estate at Rug, near Corwen, where the family had a private chapel. Bradwen was appointed organist there at eighteen, playing for the family and for public services held in the chapel. He stayed for five years and began to give recitals and formed a male voice choir in the Corwen area. Then he moved to Holyhead to be organist and choirmaster at the newer church of St Seiriol. The First World War intervened, and Bradwen Jones joined the army. He was stationed at Oswestry where he managed to maintain his music activities by playing the organ at local churches and giving recitals when the opportunity allowed.

He sailed with the expeditionary force to Egypt, where, before demobilisation, he conducted a Welsh male voice choir, composed, and played his own compositions at concerts.

On demobilisation he returned to Holyhead, and thereafter contributed considerably to the music life of the town and the surrounding area. He founded the Holyhead Musical Society and for some years he was music master at Trearddur House School. He produced Gilbert & Sullivan operas, and finally became organist at Hyfrydle chapel.

Holyhead, a town where there has always been a changing population due, no doubt, to its importance as a port, can claim several other outstanding characters who have added colour to the town's story.

I

Inns – bypassed and forgotten

The traveller taking the quiet B5109 road from Llangefni to Holyhead passes the remains of the old inn, Y Gwyndy, and can be forgiven for not noticing it. A crumbled wall stands above the road between Bodffordd and Bodedern, at Ty'n Llan, partly hidden by trees. Yet, between 1758 and the opening of Thomas Telford's new Holyhead road in 1822, it was one of the busiest places on the island for it was here that horses and riders were rested on their journey from the Beaumaris and Porthaethwy ferries to the port of Holyhead. This journey could take up to three hours along what was then the post road.

Gwyndy was referred to as a 'post office' – a place to change horses – and it was in its heyday during the era of coach travel which brought travellers from far afield to sail for Ireland, as well as mail.

The Anglesey post road was notorious for its poor condition which made travel by coach an unpleasant and dangerous experience. Passengers were assured, however, of every comfort at Gwyndy which was regarded as an upper class inn. At one time no fewer than twenty-one horses were stabled there, to serve as fresh changes for the mail coach and single riders. It was a thriving business.

In 1773 it was recorded that the inn boasted three parlours, rooms above them, a kitchen, a bar and a cellar, with a brewery and a dairy outside. There were fifteen beds.

45

The inn was leased by the landowner to an innkeeper who had to work hard to raise the rent. In 1808 he advertised in the *North Wales Gazette*:

James Knowles, Gwindy (sic). Impressed with a strong sense of the favours he has received from the Nobility, Gentry, & Travellers in general, since his own & his late Mother's occupation of the above Inn (in the whole upwards of the space of 50 years) begs leave gratefully to acknowledge his obligations . . . and whilst fulfilling this duty, permit him respectfully to inform them, that he continues in the above inn, and assures them that no exertions of his shall be wanting to render them every accommodation in his power, earnestly hoping that the length of time his family have occupied Gwindy (sic), will ensure him a continuance of those favours he has before received.

There was praise from some of the guests. Skrine, travelling to Holyhead in 1798, wrote:

Gwyndu (sic), a single house near the centre of Anglesea, where every accommodation was admirably supplied and much enhanced by the attention of our worthy old landlady, who had been fixed on the spot for over forty years.

The state of the road prompted lobbying for improvement. Various schemes were considered but it was Thomas Telford who proposed building a new road to avoid the dangerous hills and abrupt bends of the old, winding post road.

When his new road was opened in 1822, avoiding the difficult terrain of the Llandyfrydog area where Gwyndy was situated, it sounded the death knell for the old inn.

Today three ruined stone buildings, one with two huge chimney stacks, are all that remain.

The 1819 Report to the Parliamentary Commissioners regarding the new road included a claim for compensation from the owner of Gwyndy, who complained that his inn would thereafter be isolated.

There had to be a replacement. It was still the age of the coach and horses. Animals needed to be rested, as did their riders. So Telford included plans for a roadside inn at Mona to replace Gwyndy, and this opened in 1822.

Telford provided a two-storey, five-bayed range, the inn itself being in the centre of the north range in a double courtyard of buildings. Increased traffic which could now travel more safely and faster along the new road was anticipated, so accommodation was designed to meet demand. There was also ample accommodation for grooms, with coach houses and stables.

The innkeeper from Gwyndy was the first to manage the Mona Inn.

The Mona Inn's initial success was short-lived. It, too, was bypassed within a few years, not by a new road but by the railway which brought dramatic change to the way travellers to Ireland were conveyed across Anglesey.

The inn is now a farmhouse, seen to the left of the A5 road between Rhostrehwfa and Gwalchmai. It has now been bypassed for the second time, by the fast A55 expressway.

J

Justice – Beaumaris-style

The squat white courthouse opposite the castle on the main street in Beaumaris has many tales to tell of the sentences meted out to miscreants since 1617.

In early times these were harsh. Those sentenced to imprisonment were held in the castle until the town gaol was built in 1829. The courthouse remained in use until 1971. Today, both courthouse and gaol are tourist attractions. In the courthouse the visitor experiences a trial in progress through an audio presentation, with life size models of the judge, a barrister and a jury man adding reality to the sound. But that is not all. In the room beyond the court there are facsimiles of records kept through the years, quoting indictments and the sentences given to those poor men, women and children who had the misfortune to have been apprehended.

Few judges in Wales in the 17th and 18th centuries, and even later, understood Welsh. So all proceedings had to take place in English. The accused who were mainly monoglot Welsh and often poor people with little or no education were unable to plead their cases personally and understood little of what was going on. Even when the language situation improved, the conduct of court officials left much to be desired. Justice was not done.

One such occasion was the trial of the Crigyll robbers in 1740. They were a gang of men who plundered wrecks along

The remains of Gwindy at Ty'n Llan.

Nelson stands guard over the Menai Strait.

The inner harbour, Holyhead.

The Breakwater Quarry, Holyhead, now a country park.

The Skinner Monument at Morawelon, Holyhead.

One of the brown signs along Telford's Holyhead road.

The plaque commemorating William Bradwen Jones at Holyhead.

Nant y Pandy, Llangefni.

Oriel Ynys Môn, Rhosmeirch.

The Crown Inn, Bodedern.

Telford's Mona Inn, now a farmhouse.

Telford's Holyhead Road and the A55 expressway run side by side at Llanfairpwll.

Plas Newydd.

William Owen Stanley's tomb at St.Cybi's church, Holyhead.

The Skerries.

The David Hughes Village Hall, Cemaes.

The Britannia Bridge memorial, Llanfairpwll.

Tŷ Coch, the home of Sir John Morris Jones at Llanfairpwll.

The Morris Borthers memorial at Brynrefail.

The Toll House, Llanfairpwll.

The Prichard-Jones Institute.

Memorial to the Royal Charter.

The Anglesey Hunt meet outside the tollhouse at Llanfairpwll.

The tollbooth at Pont y Borth.

Beuamaris court house.

63

Anglesey county gaol at Beaumaris.

the south-west coast of Anglesey, an act which was against the law. Four of the ring-leaders were caught and brought to trial at Beaumaris. The judge was drunk. The robbers had hired a brilliant lawyer who succeeded in confusing the judge and gaining the sympathy of the jury. The robbers mustered their supporters to ring the courthouse on the day of the trial. They demanded an acquittal, which was granted.

Beaumaris court gained such a poor reputation among merchants and sea captains who suffered wrecked and plundered cargoes that one of them insisted a trial should take place in Shrewsbury where a fairer hearing could be expected.

Physical torture was practised by way of punishment. In 1737 an old woman from Llangaffo was charged with stealing forty shillings and John David, a miller of Frogwy, of killing his maid. The old woman 'having committed no burglary and being the first offence, was burnt in the hand. The miller was found guilty of manslaughter and likewise burnt in the hand'. Yet John Pritchard had been indicted for burglary and felony, and found guilty. He was hanged.

Another instance of burning is recorded seven years later, when twelve-years old Hugh Hughes was charged with accidentally killing a youth of sixteen 'by a stroak (sic) on his head with a stick'. And John Rowlands, for 'assisting and abiding him by giving him a stick and bidding him strike him.' They were tried, and both burnt in the hand, the boy 'with a cold iron' – as though this mitigated the act.

Another more serious offender, a thief: 'was burnt in earnest, the iron burning halfway through his hand.'

Reading the records it would seem that more value was put on wordly goods than on human life. In 1719 a seventeen years old boy was found guilty of stealing a horse. He was hanged.

Anne Williams stole clothes from a house at Llannerch-y-medd while the family was at chapel. She took two cotton nightdresses, a pair of stays and a silk handkerchief. Her sentence was seven years' transportation to Australia.

After the prison was built, hard labour became a common form of punishment for both sexes and even for children. Gaynor Jones was found guilty of stealing a quart of milk by catching a sheep in a field and milking into a bucket. She spent one month with hard labour in Beaumaris gaol. In 1849 Robert Hughes stole a pint of gooseberries worth one penny from a garden. He was sentenced to two months' hard labour in 'The House of Correction' (Beaumaris Gaol).

During the 1860s a poor Irish community settled in Brynsiencyn. Bridget Reilly had been caught 'handling a pocket watch'. Pregnant, she had been held in prison for two months pending trial and she was then sentenced to two more months. She gave birth to her baby girl in prison, but records show that the baby died there.

In 1888 John Smith, a well known pickpocket on the Irish ferries working as a member of a gang, appeared in court accused of stealing a purse, £2 and a penknife. He was sentenced to nine months' hard labour which would probably have included working the treadwheel which today's visitors can see still in position in the gaol.

Even children under ten years of age received similar punishment. Age was no excuse. In 1870 eight year old James Casey, no doubt driven to crime through poverty and hunger, stole half a pound of sugar and some bread and butter from John Roberts of Llannerch-y-medd, for which he was given two weeks' hard labour at the gaol 'and whipped with six strokes of the birch' which was a bundle of long, springy birch twigs.

Poverty probably drove Thomas Owen, a child of unstated age, to steal four eggs from Thomas Lewis Humphreys of Llangaffo, for which he was sentenced to 'three weeks in the House of Correction in Beaumaris Gaol'.

Afterwards he was incarcerated in a reform school for five years.

Children were cruelly treated on occasions. In 1846 Captain William Peck of the ship 'Athelston' was accused, with the mate, William Goodhill, of the murder of John Martin, a boy seaman. The child, said to be in poor health, was late arriving on deck at five a.m. to begin his duties. The mate handled him roughly and ducked him in seawater for five minutes. The captain then 'beat him with a knotted rope and a boathook and left him exposed on deck', where John later died.

The jury rejected the murder accusation and pronounced a verdict of manslaughter. Peck was imprisoned for two years, but the mate was acquitted.

One of the most famous cases to be heard at Beaumaris courthouse was probably that of Dic Rolant, a labourer, who had murdered his father-in-law in 1862. The case was given wide publicity. On the day the trial opened the local newspaper reported 'there was a great rush made to the doors which were almost carried by storm . . . the court was crammed in every part with well-dressed persons and hundreds remained outside, unable to obtain admission'. Dic Rolant pleaded not guilty but the court judged otherwise. His was the last execution to take place at Beaumaris gaol and the excuse for a public holiday in the town. Visitors filled the guest houses. The ferries across to Anglesey did a brisk trade, bringing the curious to Beaumaris and ferrying away those who did not wish to be part of the ghoulish atmosphere.

Beaumaris courthouse has certainly witnessed some heart-rending stories of poverty, cruelty and hatred.

There is a small room to one side of the main chamber of the courthouse where the accused would wait to be taken into court. A life sized model, shabbily dressed, sits waiting. This is the most awe-inspiring room in the building. The atmosphere of dread is still palpable, so many years on.

K

Keeping nature natural

Keeping nature natural is the aim of all conservationists. Nowhere is this more evident than in Anglesey, where several reserves exist to tempt the visitor to appreciate what the island has to offer in terms of fauna and flora and, at the same time, conserve for the future.

Much of this work is done by the North Wales Wildlife Trust. The purchase of three farm holdings at Cors Goch, a base-rich fen near Pentraeth, in 1964 led to the formation of the Trust. These holdings have now been extended. Today Cors Goch is of international importance as it supports so many rare plants. Volunteers help to carry out the work of managing the reserve, using traditional methods of grazing with ponies and cattle, reed cutting, hay-making, scrub clearing and burning.

Cors Goch is a marshy area, with bordering grassland. A public footpath meanders through the reserve, where visitors can expect to find rushes, sedges, reeds, orchids, many different invertebrates, over twenty butterfly species and twelve species of dragonfly.

The Mariandyrys reserve covers fifteen acres of a small hill on the eastern tip of Anglesey near Glanrafon. This is the place to see over thirty species of birds. The area covered by the reserve is designated common land for the extraction of firewood, although this right is rarely exercised these days, and is leased to the Trust. As at Cors Goch, butterflies are very numerous, with around twenty species and over eighty species of moth having been recorded here. Habitats at Mariandyrys vary from a small quarry, woodland, heathland, to grassland.

Nearby is the common land at Llanddona, one of Anglesey's several Local Nature Reserves (LNRs), a council responsibility. This is unique, as it consists of a patchwork of open areas dotted around the village of Llanddona and connected by paths and roads. Commons rights to graze cattle belonging to the villagers were exercised, it is believed, until about thirty years ago. Since then scrub and rank growth have taken over. There are plans for the future of Llanddona with the aim being to restore and maintain heathland habitat while retaining the diversity of habitat and plant communities.

Llanddona common consists of dry heathland, scrub, underscrub and grassland. There are good bird nesting sites in gorse and bramble.

In the mid 1990s Caeau Pen y Clip, on the outskirts of Menai Bridge, were donated to the Wales Wildlife Trust. This is a series of small fields close to housing, which provide an important refuge for wildlife close to the town, but edged by agricultural land. There are hedgerows providing food and shelter for birds and insects. The Trust uses winter grazing to maintain the grassland but in the summer wild flowers are allowed to bloom unhindered. The wetter areas are good places to see frogs, newts and dragonflies.

Holy Island has the Porth Diana nature reserve, south of Trearddur Bay. This is part of the nationally important coastal heath on the west coast of the island, where dry heath and damp grassland are two habitats.

The North Wales Wildlife Trust's Cemlyn reserve is leased by them from the National Trust. It has the only substantial colony of Sandwich terns in Wales, with large numbers of Common and Arctic terns and a few pairs of the rare Roseate tern. Winter is the time to see impressive numbers of wildfowl on the lagoon.

The Cemlyn lagoon was managed as a private wildfowl refuge for more than forty years by the resident of Bryn Aber, Col. Vivian Hewitt. After his death the Cemlyn estate was bought by the National Trust who leased part of it as a nature reserve to the Wildlife Trust. The lagoon was built in the 1930s, so converting mud flats into a permanent stretch of water whose height is regulated by the weir. The shingle ridge and around the fringes of the lagoon, and the islands in the water, are home to a wide variety of plants.

Visitors are urged to follow and obey the signs at Cemlyn, and are asked not to walk along the crest or the lagoon side of the ridge from May to mid August, as this could disturb nesting activity. During the winter the best vantage points to view wildfowl are from the roads to the south-west and west of the lagoon.

Details of all the Anglesey nature reserves – pamphlets, maps and information – can be had at Tourist Information Centres and from the head office of the Trust in Bangor. Some of the larger reserves have wardens on hand during the summer, to meet visitors and point out the features of interest.

Anglesey has one public park, in Holyhead, but a recent development at Llangefni provides a similar amenity. This is an LNR managed by Anglesey County Council's Countryside Service.

Nant y Pandy is a twenty-five acre wooded valley, a steep sided gorge bisected by the river Cefni. Known by some as The Dingle, Nant y Pandy is its Welsh name and used by the Council to advertise its amenities. This name refers to the stream of the fulling mill, the remains of which can be seen upstream. The entrance to Nant y Pandy is close by the parish church of St Cyngar near the town centre and marked by some modern sculpture. This area has been enhanced through community involvement, working in partnership and by grant aid. A wooden boardwalk has been laid; there are three new bridges over the river, and benches and picnic tables put up for the use of visitors. The boardwalk allows access to many parts of the reserve where glimpses of wildlife can be enjoyed.

Careful observation has to be maintained on all nature reserves which are not without their problems. At the time of writing, Himalayan Balsam, already classed as a pest by the government, is appearing at Nant y Pandy. It is encroaching on the woodland and competing with native plants. But prompt and thorough action is being taken to destroy the pest and so halt the invasion.

The Holyhead Breakwater Country Park was opened in 1990. It is the site of the old quarry which supplied stone for the building of the breakwater. Pathways lead through gorse and heather, high above the sea. There are moorhens and mallards on Llyn Llwynog, and choughs and peregrine falcons swoop above the old quarry. The park has an interpretive centre, a shop and a café. This Country Park is managed by Ynys Môn County Council.

The largest area of nature reserve on the island is that beyond Newborough, including the Warren and the Forest, which is managed by the Countryside Council for Wales. While encouraging visitors, the Council is highly aware of the problems they can cause to a sensitive environment, and the co-operation of those visitors in helping to maintain the right balance is constantly urged. This is an area rich in so much – flora, fauna, the beach at Llanddwyn, the development of the forest – and it is one of Anglesey's greatest treasures.

There are other smaller reserves and places of natural interest on the island – Ellin's Tower Seabird Centre operated by the RSPB perched on the cliffs overlooking

South Stack is one. The RSPB can also give information about its bird hides elsewhere on the island. Llyn Alaw is the large reservoir in the centre of Anglesey which has pathways along its shores. The Mill Race Woodland in Beaumaris is managed by the County Council's Countryside Service.

The North Wales Wildlife Trust, Ynys Môn County Council, Menter Môn and the Countryside Commission publicise the existing LNRs. There are four others in the pipeline for the near future. All are diligent guardians of Anglesey's precious natural life.

Anglesey schools are encouraging a growing interest among young people in the importance of the wildlife in their own locality. If this can be maintained and fostered there is every hope of keeping nature natural on the island.

L

Lost cargoes

Looking into the story of shipping around the Anglesey coast, especially during the days of sail, one is struck by the number of wrecks which must litter the sea bed. By the mid-19th century the Irish Sea had become one of the most important shipping lanes to and from Britain with Liverpool being the premier west coast port from Chester and Parkgate.

The newly inaugurated lifeboat service saved hundreds of lives but loss of precious cargoes from the merchant ships was a serious problem.

One of the early wrecks recorded was that of the first Royal yacht, 'Mary', in March 1675. She had been found inappropriate for royal use and was relegated to providing transport for important personages to and from Ireland. 'Mary' was wrecked close to the Skerries while on a voyage home from Ireland with thirty-nine passengers and crew. Most managed to reach land safely, but the ship sank and for several centuries remained forgotten until a chance dive by Lancashire sub aqua club members in 1971 located two of her bronze guns. From that date the research was stepped up, and today nearly 1500 objects from the wreck lie safely in the care of the Maritime Museum in Liverpool, including guns, an anchor, coins, tableware and jewellery.

A vast amount of commercial cargo has been lost over the years.

Animals were difficult to deal with in bad weather, and had little hope of survival if a ship was wrecked.

In 1842 a wooden paddle steamer, 'Monk', sailing from Porthdinllaen to Liverpool with a cargo of butter and 140 pigs, missed the tide at the entrance to the Menai Strait, a notoriously difficult and dangerous passage which had to be timed to the minute. She stranded and broke up. Lives were lost and the bodies of the crew who did not manage to escape and the drowned pigs were washed ashore at Fort Belan on the Caernarfonshire coast by the next tide.

In the winter of 1868, 'Town of Wexford' was sailing to Liverpool carrying livestock. She anchored off Trefadog during a storm, where her anchor parted and she went ashore. Holyhead lifeboat crew saved all forty-three passengers and crew, but nothing could be done to save the cargo. The next day local people saw the pitiful sight of dead cattle and pigs floating on the water.

In the days of emigration to America, space taken by emigrants on the outward journey was often used by cattle on the return voyage to Britain. In 1897 the Dominion Line 'Angloman' hit the West Platters off the Skerries. Four lifeboats sped to take off seventy passengers and crew, but 700 cattle and 1500 sheep perished in the wreck.

In October 1859 one of the most violent storms of the century hit the coast of Britain on a night when hundreds of ships foundered.

'Royal Charter', a large iron steam clipper, was on her way from Australia to Liverpool with 390 passengers, many of whom had been successful in the Australian Gold Rush and were bringing home their acquired wealth. The ship also carried bullion worth well over £300,000.

The hurricane hit her as she sailed into Liverpool Bay, almost at the end of her long voyage, and she was swept by gigantic seas on to the rocks at Porth Helaeth, near Moelfre. No rescue could be attempted and local people watched helplessly as the ship broke up, spilling men, women and children into the sea where most were pounded to death on the rocks.

As there was so much valuable cargo the Crown enlisted the help of twenty local men to collect the gold and valuables washed ashore. Subsequent dives have brought to the surface artefacts from 'Royal Charter' which can be seen in the Maritime Museum at Liverpool and the Seawatch Centre at Moelfre, but much still remains to be examined under water. The sea keeps its secrets well.

The First World War found German U-boats patrolling the Irish Sea, lurking to attack shipping. S.S. 'Cambank' was torpedoed off Point Lynas in 1915 when a large amount of copper was lost as the ship went down. Forty years later this valuable cargo was brought to the surface.

The Second World War also saw casualties in the Irish Sea. Lighthouses were unlit for a time. In 1943 the Ellerman Lines 'Castellan' was hit by a severe storm in Church Bay. Her anchor failed to hold and she ran on to the East Platters where she wedged. The crew of forty-seven jumped to the safety of the Holyhead lifeboat just as the ship sank in 100 feet of water, taking her cargo of copper and explosives with her.

Not all the cargoes of wrecked ships sank beneath the waves, however. Some were lost through stealth.

Where Afon Crigyll enters the sea north of Rhosneigr it does so through an area of marsh land and dunes, sparsely populated and ideal for nefarious practices. Cornish Lamping was once practised here. This was a method invented to attract sailing ships to their doom by hanging lighted lamps around the necks of grazing cattle to simulate undulating lights of ships in harbour, so that unwary ships would be enticed close in to shore, at their peril.

This practice was forbidden, but enthusiastically supported nevertheless, as Cymyran Bay was a remote spot where revenue cutters rarely patrolled.

Thankfully, frequent shipwrecks no longer occur, with the advent of navigational aids. But the Irish Sea still holds its secrets.

M

Meeting the people

There have been many travellers to Anglesey who have left written accounts of their experiences. They have deplored the state of the roads, praised the glorious scenery, criticised or applauded the services received in inns and hotels. But the most readable are those who have recorded meeting the people, for it takes people to bring a period and a place to life.

George Borrow was the socialiser par excellence. However irritating his supercilious attitude, his conversations breathe life into the word pictures he paints of the places he visited and the people he met.

Borrow set out on a pilgrimage to find Llanfair Mathafarn Eithaf, the birthplace of the poet he admired, Goronwy Owen. Not knowing the way, he accosted an old man in Upper Bangor who was amazed that 'a Saxon' should speak Welsh. Borrow was directed to the Menai suspension bridge, where the tollkeeper pointed towards Four Crosses, and instructed him to make for it then turn towards Pentraeth. There he sought refreshment at 'The White House' and met the publican, Hugh Pritchard:

> . . . a tall, bulky man with a weather-beaten countenance, dressed in a brown jerkin and corduroy trowsers (sic), with a broad low-crowned buff-coloured hat on his head, and what might be called half shoes and half high-lows

on his feet. He had a short pipe in his mouth which when he greeted me he took out, but replaced as soon as the greeting was over, which consisted of 'Good day, sir' delivered in a frank hearty tone. I looked Mr Hugh Pritchard in the face and thought I had never seen a more honest countenance.

In conversation with the maid, Borrow learned that the family had left Liverpool to take possession of the inn.

Borrow had an opportunity to boast of his ability to read Welsh poetry when he met the miller of Llanfair Mathafarn Eithaf. Poor though the family may have been, the miller and his wife persuaded Borrow to take tea with them. He was touched by their hospitality, especially when the miller's wife opened a cupboard to produce 'a basin of snow-white lump sugar, and taking the spoon out of my hand, placed two of the largest lumps in my cup though she helped neither her husband nor herself; the sugar-basin probably being kept solely for grand occasions . . . ' . Borrow then had the grace to admit: 'My eyes filled with tears; for in the whole course of my life I had never experienced so much genuine hospitality.'

Borrow's introduction to Mr Bos, the drover, at the Pentraeth Inn, produced a very different reaction:

. . . He was a man seemingly about forty years of age with a broad red face, with certain somethings, looking very much like incipient carbuncles, here and there upon it. His eyes were grey and looked rather as if they squinted; his mouth was very wide, and when it opened displayed a set of strong white, uneven teeth. He was dressed in a pepper and salt coat of the Newmarket cut, breeches of corduroy and brown top boots, and had on his head a broad, black, coarse, low crowned hat. In his left hand he held a heavy white whalebone whip with a brass head.

Here, Borrow met his match as far as boasting was concerned, but he did compare him unfavourably with the innkeeper. When making his farewells Borrow told Hugh Pritchard: 'You have a fault which will always prevent your rising in this world, you have modesty; those who have modesty shall have no advancement, whilst those who can blow their own horn lustily shall be made governors.'

Francis Kilvert, the clerical diarist from Herefordshire, visited Anglesey briefly in 1871. He, too, was directed to Four Crosses and records his guide:

As we crossed the bridge and were approaching the Anglesey shore we overtook a quaint, humorous old man with a tall white hat, a merry twinkle in his eye, and a huge cancer in his face. I fell into talk with him. 'Now', he said as we left the bridge and walked into Anglesey, 'now you are like Robinson Crusoe, you are on your island. How should you like to live in that house all the year round, winter and summer?' he said, pointing to a white house on a little rock island in the straits. I said I thought there might be worse places. 'They live like fighting cocks there' winked the old man with a merry twinkle in his eye and his tall white hat nodding from side to side. 'They have got a weir there and they catch all the fish'.

He was referring, of course, to Gorad Goch, in between the two bridges, with its fish weir.

Dean Jonathan Swift, grumbler of note and apparently one of the most irascible of men, made the journey to Ireland through Holyhead in April 1727. In those days, being under sail, voyages were erratic and subject to delay depending on the weather. Company aboard was not to Swift's liking, as he recalls in his Journal:

I should be glad to talk with Farmers and Shopkeepers but none of them speak English. A Dog is better company than the Vicar, for I remember him of old . . . The Master of the packet-boat, one Jones, hath not treated me with the least civility although Watt gave him my name. In short I come from being used like an Emperor to be used worse than a Dog at Holyhead. Yet my hat is worn to pieces by answering the civilities of the poor inhabitants as they pass by.

In his *Sketches in Wales*, written in 1826, George Freeman was more pleasantly disposed to the packet service. He watched the ferry being prepared for departure and wrote:

Captain P. himself afforded us some amusement. That gentleman had the appearance of a right merry fellow when he pleased, but never without recollections of office. His air was authoritative, his voice loud and quick, and his orders were obeyed on board and ashore, as though they were the fiat of destiny. He moved his chapeau to all strangers who were well dressed, and familiarly shook hands with old acquaintances. Exactly at half past six, he sung out, with watch in hand: 'Is all aboard?' and receiving affirmative reply, he ordered the vessel to be shoved off.

Lady travellers, too, kept diaries of their visits. Mrs Thrale, in the company of Dr Johnson, found Beaumaris to her liking, and while there met the schoolmaster who offered to be their guide:

We walked with our new friend to Baron Hill, the seat of Lord Bulkeley, a place of beautiful situation commanding the Castle, the Streights (sic), and the mountains, an assemblage scarcely to be mended even by the imagination. We spent some time among the woods and the walks and proceeded to a Castle of no small dignity or extent, yet much unknown to the talking World ... the gentleman was desirous of showing Mr Johnson his School and so he did.

Augusta Pearson, in *A Spinster's Tour through North Wales*, tells of her visit to Beaumaris, too. While there she made the trip to Penmon and 'from thence we went to the Lighthouse close to Puffin Island off which the 'Rothsay Castle' a steamer from Liverpool was lost. [This referred to a tragic ship-wreck on the Lavan Sands which had prompted Trinity House to build the lighthouse at Trwyn Du, which first showed a light in 1838.] We had some talk with the lighthouse man who seemed to have a very snug berth there, a most comfortable looking house with a nice Garden, but he was evidently one of the dissatisfied ones of this world and complained much of the extreme loneliness, though there were two men employed there and plenty to do,' she commented.

Augusta had an answer to his problem: 'I recommended him strongly to get a wife to make it cheerful, but he only shook his head at my advice,' she wrote with tongue in cheek.

When Richard Warner made his *Second Walk through Wales* in 1798 he chose to cross to Anglesey by the Garth Point ferry, operated by a 'singular character' named Grace Parry. He described her as:

A short thick, squat female who, though upwards of sixty

winters have passed over her head, is as strong as a horse and as active as one of her own country goats.

Grace Parry was plain-spoken, fearless, was Welsh to the core and made her preferences known. There was no shilly-shallying with Grace Parry. Richard Warner and his travelling companion soon had her measure:

As we found Grace's prejudices against the English were rather violent, and not knowing to what length they might carry her, particularly when she was under the influence of 'cwrw da', we thought it necessary for the safety of future Saxon travellers, to reward her labours with double the sum she demanded. This unexpected generosity so gratified the old woman that she swore most bitterly we were the 'greatest gentlemen' she ever met with; she declared, she should always like the English for our sake, and insisted on shaking hands with us individually at parting. We indulged her wish (whether she meant it as a token of her kindness or a proof of her strength I know not), gave us each such a serious grip as almost dislocated our fingers.

John Wesley visited Anglesey several times, on his way to Ireland. When the weather delayed sea crossings he would grasp the opportunity to preach or to attend a church service although making contact was difficult because of the language barrier. One Sunday in 1748 he recorded in his Journal:

We went to Llangefni church, though we understood little of what we heard. Oh, what a heavy curse was the confusion of tongues! And how grievous are the effects of it! All the birds of the air, all the beasts of the field, understand the language of their own species. Man only is a barbarian to man, unintelligible to his own brethren.

John Wesley might have made a greater impact, and been enriched, had he made the effort as did George Borrow half a century later, to learn some Welsh!

N

Newborough's rush matting industry

The stranger to Newborough, the small village behind the sand dunes of south-west Anglesey, might think that agriculture has been its only industry. Yet it once had another, which grew out of the necessity to eke out a living by the poverty-stricken population.

The raw material was marram grass which grows profusely in the sand. It was harvested to plait mats to cover haystacks and barn roofs, and to make nets and cordage for fishermen.

What is now referred to as Newborough Warren and Newborough Forest is one of the largest dune areas in Britain. During the 14th century great storms blew sand inland to build up the dune complex, an area of ever-shifting sand which needed to be restrained if it was not to engulf the surrounding farmland even more. During the reign of Elizabeth I laws were passed to forbid the destruction of marram grass, as it was realised that this was an important ground-stabilising factor.

It is not known when mat-making began. Traditionally it was women's work, done at home to add to the low wages of the men working on the land, but as demand for these hard-wearing mats grew, the whole family would be involved. A local historian, commenting on the busiest period in this domestic industry, writes of every house being like a small factory 'supplying not only the district around but even parts of Caernarvonshire, Denbighshire and Flintshire'.

The skills were regarded as hereditary, or learned when the worker was very young. Those coming to it late in life, it was said, were all fingers and thumbs and produced inferior results.

When the Enclosures Acts put land into the hands of private owners they began to charge for harvesting, and eventually rented plots to the villagers.

The grass was harvested during late August or early September, using a broad-bladed reaping hook which cut the grass below the sand but just above the root, leaving a stool from which the grass could grow again for the following season, and not affecting its stabilising use.

The cut grass was left to ripen as it was spread out to dry in a sheltered spot in the dunes where wind and sun would make it hard, dry and white.

The reeds were then bundled, with the useless grey stalks first removed, and the bundles collected into sheaves to be stored at home.

Although this was mainly a domestic craft, if there happened to be an empty building in the village some women would meet together and enjoy village gossip while mat-making.

The mats consisted of plaited strips of grass, sewn together. Each completed mat consisted of sixteen plaits in width, four 'Welsh' yards in length – a 'Welsh' yard measured forty inches.

Mats were sold through a barter system. A worker would buy food from the local grocer or butcher, paying in mats. Merchants travelled the district, bought the mats from the tradesmen and took them to the fairs at Cricieth and Pwllheli where farmers would buy them, and they were also bought locally. The worker was usually given food valued at around 1/10d for each mat bartered, the shopkeeper selling on as a middleman to the merchant for 3/-, so making a good profit.

Newborough people also made rope from marram grass, useful on the farms but also for packing glassware and pottery and for packing barbed wire for transportation.

Then came a change. Colonel Stapleton-Cotton retired from the army and went to live in a house on the Plas Newydd estate where he had family connections. He was an Edwardian entrepreneur, better known countrywide for being the founder of the Women's Institute in Britain. He contributed a great deal to the economy of south Anglesey by experimenting successfully with several business projects. He regarded the Newborough mat-making industry as a failing proposition which had possibilities. It had little or no marketing structure, in his opinion, the bartering being almost medieval. So he formed the Newborough Mat-Makers Association. He searched for new markets to ensure that there would be continuing use for the workers' skills, albeit sometimes in a different direction. Those who joined the Association began to produce strawberry mats, floor mats and baskets as well as mats for covering haystacks. By the end of the First World War the Association was a thriving concern. There was a depot in the village for storing materials and finished articles. The old bartering system vanished and workers in the 1920s received 3/- for every mat they delivered to the depot and reasonable pay for other articles. The business structure proved its worth.

Time brought further changes. By the 1930s demand had dwindled. Skills had disappeared as young people moved away to find work elsewhere. Marram grass mat-making was becoming an art form only.

Today only one worker remains who is skilled in the craft. The last marram grass plaiter in Newborough has an arrangement with the Countryside Council to collect bundles of the grass from the dunes. Is this traditional skill to be allowed to disappear without some effort being made to continue it? It is to be hoped it can be rescued, even if only as an art form. Anglesey cannot afford to lose the tradition.

O

Oriel treasures

Anglesey's newest treasure – Oriel Ynys Môn at Llangefni –
houses some of the island's oldest treasures. But it also looks
forward to the future.

The purpose-built museum and gallery on the hill at
Rhosmeirch, north of the town, was built against a
background of controversy in that some criticised the use of
public money for such an ambitious venture at that time.
However, built it was, and opened by HM The Queen in
1991. It has since proved its worth to such an extent that the
critics have been won over, and it is now the centre of
cultural activity in Anglesey.

The undoubted success of the Oriel can be attributed to
an enthusiastic and dedicated staff, under its curator, Alun
Gruffydd, who work ceaselessly within a strict budget, and
provide a service which would be the pride of any county.

On opening, the Oriel inherited some treasures, and has
since acquired others.

A core collection of pictures, archaeological finds and
other artefacts previously in the hands of 'Cyngor Gwlad
Môn' before the demise of that body, became their
responsibility.

The premises are divided into two similarly sized
galleries, one housing a comprehensive Heritage section. Its
twin is the home of art and craft displays which change
frequently, some from the Oriel's own extensive stock,

others the work of local contemporary artists and craftspeople, and, occasionally, a national travelling exhibition.

The Oriel was built at the time the then local Council had acquired a substantial collection of pictures by local artist C.F. Tunnicliffe who came from Cheshire late in life to settle at Malltraeth, where he studied and drew and painted the bird life of Anglesey. One of the Oriel's treasures is a collection of 360 of his drawings and paintings, including all the black and white drawings he made for the many books he illustrated, and the original plate for one of these.

In the Heritage gallery visitors can see a reproduction of his studio at Malltraeth, his bench with brushes and colours ready to be used, his spectacles nearby ready to be worn. Tunnicliffe's pictures are displayed from time to time in the art gallery. Rarely would one find such a concentrated effort to highlight the work of a local artist in a museum and gallery, but with such a proliferation of talent this is no surprise.

Anglesey, as every art lover knows, is the home of Sir Kyffin Williams, so it is appropriate that the Oriel has a valuable collection of Wales's most well-known contemporary artist's work in its possession, including many of his arresting portraits of local characters which add yet another dimension to the importance of the collection as far as Anglesey is concerned.

The third of the three major art collections here is that of the two Massey sisters whose botanical studies, as well as being beautiful works of art in themselves, are also a comprehensive illustrated record of the flora to be seen during the early years of the 20th century on Anglesey.

The Heritage gallery, which is to be re-organised when funds allow, consists of well-planned sections dealing with various aspects of Anglesey's history throughout the ages.

This gives opportunity to display such treasures as

archaeological finds from earliest times. There are several items from the Iron Age hoard found at Llyn Cerrig Bach when the runway at RAF Valley was being extended. Most of the finds are at the National Museum of Wales in Cardiff, but these precious smaller-items did not find their way there with the main hoard, and are jealously appreciated on the island where they were found.

Some of the archaeological finds are on loan from owners who have treasured them but wish to share them with others.

Geology is remembered on an island which boasts some of the oldest rocks in the world. Specimens have come from the Anglesey Antiquarian Society & Field Club. Another collection has been given to the Oriel by a local man who had collected his specimens as a youth.

A recent treasure came to light at Llanfairpwll, when a hedge around a farmhouse gatepost was trimmed to reveal a figurehead cemented into the stone post. The Hendy head, as it is now known, believed to be of ancient origin, has posed some problems as to its exact age to expert archaeologists even. It is now in the Heritage gallery of the Oriel, a face with an enigmatic smile, giving no secrets away. A unique treasure.

The sea has always been part of Anglesey life. Everyone knows the tragic story of the wreck of 'Royal Charter' in 1859. On her way from Australia to Liverpool during Gold Rush days, she was wrecked during a night of unprecedented storms off Moelfre.

Most of the artefacts which came to shore or were later lifted from the sea can be seen at the Maritime Museum in Liverpool, but Oriel Ynys Môn has a few poignant reminders, such as a tiny shoe belonging to one of the hapless children lost on that terrible night. A tiny shoe, a tiny treasure.

A worthwhile museum never rests on its laurels. Alun Gruffydd and his staff acknowledge that history is being made today and will be made tomorrow, next week, next month, next year. Change should be recorded as it happens. Local artists are supported through frequent exhibitions of their work. They draw and paint local scenes, recording landscape, buildings, people and events on the island which are ever-changing.

During 2004 the Oriel mounted an exhibition showing the development of the A55 expressway across Anglesey, how it affected local communities, and in particular the archaeological treasures found during excavations.

Bringing history to light during the 21st century will be one of the aims of the Oriel. Who knows what treasures will be unearthed in coming years?

P

Passing the message

As buildings have fallen into decay, evidence of a unique system which once operated between Anglesey and Liverpool, has almost been obliterated. But written evidence remains, from which it is possible to recreate the story.

In the days of sailing ships, when the Irish Sea began to take on special importance as one of the main shipping lines in and out of Britain through the port of Liverpool, many shipowners were Liverpool men living close enough to the Mersey shore to be able to use a telescope from a window to scan the river for their ships. It was also used for reading messages conveyed by house flags hoisted, when appropriate, on Bidston Hill as well as far out into Liverpool Bay and on a clear day across to the coast of Wales.

The Bidston Hill flag poles whose positions could still be glimpsed long after they had gone out of use were ranged in a line from north to south, dozens of them at one time when the volume of shipping was at its highest. The signals were read by a watchman in Liverpool and messages delivered by runners to the nearby Merchants' coffee house where shipowners met when in town on business.

As the port of Liverpool grew, so did competition for berths, and it was seen that a new signalling system was needed so that owners could make adequate arrangements for approaching vessels, prior to their arrival at Liverpool.

In June 1825 an Act of Parliament authorised and empowered Liverpool Dock Trustees:

> . . . to establish a speedy mode of communication to the ship owners and merchants at Liverpool of the arrival of ships and vessels off the Port of Liverpool on the coast of Wales, by building, erecting and maintaining signal houses, telegraphs or such other mode of communication as to them shall seem expedient, between Liverpool and Hoylake or between Liverpool and the Isle of Anglesea.

Eleven signal stations along the coast from Holyhead to the Wirral were proposed. Operators had to have a clear view to the previous station and to the next along the line. The first station was built at the extreme western end of Anglesey, about five hundred feet above sea level between North and South Stack. This station picked up flag signals from passing ships and relayed messages by semaphore to the next station at Church Bay.

About ten miles east of Church Bay, three hundred feet above the coast line and overlooking Point Lynas, the Llaneilian station was built. This was especially important because it was where the Mersey pilots took over to enter Liverpool or were dropped as ships left the Bay.

Thirteen miles from there was Ynys Seiriol. If ever there was an inhospitable, lonely station, this was it, although it was ideally situated to pass on signals from Llaneilian to the next in line, on the top of the Great Orme at Llandudno.

The signal stations were small buildings of one storey, like small observatories. Each had a huge signal mast rising up through the roof.

The total cost for the 72-mile stretch was estimated to be £1,300 for the eleven buildings, £100 for telescopes and £300 for plans and to superintend the erection of the stations.

This was the first telegraph system to be installed by a

public body. The Holyhead line operators were not experts when the system first began, so a simple system of coding had to be planned. This was done by Lieutenant Barnard Lindsay Watson who had designed the route. He published his code in book form. A copy now lies in the Liverpool Central Library.

The semaphore messages were relayed on identical masts at each station. The arms were made of African oak and painted black so that they could be seen more clearly. Each was about 7½ft long by 16" wide, fitted into a groove in the lower part of the mast. Three pairs of these worked on three separate pivots, and they were worked into their different positions by being hauled up by ropes passing through blocks in the 40-50ft high mast. At the end of each rope was an iron weight like a bolt, which balanced the arms and fitted into holes in the mast at exact points so that the arms could be raised to the required positions. This enabled the operator to work the signals from inside his observation room without having to see the arms.

The positions of the arms were numbered, 1 to 9. The code of signals allowed for all contingencies. For instance, the group of figures 832 signified 'bad news'; 840 was 'bags of cotton'; 972 indicated 'belonging to this port'; 80 was 'lost her boat'; 83 was 'send boats to our assistance'; 467 indicated 'melancholy catastrophe' and 804 'contagious disease'.

Watson also strung together what he called a list of verbs. 'Let me be' was 432; 'can I do', 653. Compass signals were given numbers, presumably for additions.

The telegraph stations themselves had numbers, too – Holyhead was 50. Pilot signals which were hoisted on the crosstree of the mast by flags indicated messages like 'carry all the sail you can', or 'a lifeboat is coming alongside'.

The book listed several regulations which ships' masters had to observe. Homeward bound vessels had to show their number immediately they came in sight of the Holyhead station and keep it flying until answered from the telegraph station on shore. 'By this means a pilot boat will have immediate intelligence of the vessel being off shore long before she can be seen', the manual explained.

It continued:

All vessels for Liverpool, on getting to the eastwards of a line from the rock called The Middle Mouse, are liable to a fine of £5 if neglecting to hoist a signal for a pilot and keep it flying until they have got one on board, and are also liable to pay pilotage if they refuse or neglect taking the first pilot that offers within that line . . . Outward bound vessels which carry their number when they leave dock and out of the river will be reported to Holyhead as having sailed, and a constant look out will be kept for them along the line and their progress reported in Liverpool as occasion may require.

There was a lookout man on duty at each station throughout the hours of daylight. This must have been reassuring to ships off the coast who would know that help could be summoned instantly if they were in danger.

The signal system gave regular information about the weather and wind force, so that ships leaving Liverpool would know what to expect when rounding Anglesey into the Irish Sea.

The operators became adept at working their appliances. Messages were sent by groups of numbers and eventually they could send them so quickly that often the first group would have arrived at Liverpool by the time the last group was leaving Holyhead. A short message could travel the length of the line, and an answer returned, all in 53 seconds – so the system gained the reputation of being 'faster than the wind'.

It was a rule that signals should be kept as brief as

possible and made only if absolutely necessary. Watson's rules stated:

All frivolous or useless communication should be avoided as it can tend to no good purpose and may occupy the telegraph when intelligence of importance at some other part of the line is waiting to be communicated.

However, there is the story of an operator at Holyhead in 1830 who became exasperated with another down the line who was slow in his responses to signals. So he signalled the relevant number code YOU ARE STUPID; and back came the answer YOU ARE DISMISSED. Unknown to the Holyhead operator, his overseer was receiving at the next station!

In 1833 Lieutenant Watson submitted a progress report, in which he claimed that over 1,300 ships using the semaphore system were on his list, and all the messages had been transmitted to Liverpool within a few minutes.

In 1839 Lieutenant William Lord was appointed superintendent in Watson's place and further improvements to the system began right away. The Church Bay station was augmented by a new one at Cefn Du, near Llanrhyddlad, which enabled one to be used if the other was in mist. More substantial buildings were built and some of these are now pleasant small homes and listed buildings. The tall masts were replaced by twin lattice posts of wrought iron, each with two pairs of arms, which stood on the roof of the observation room. William Lord also introduced a new, extended code.

The 1850s saw experiments with an electric telegraph, as the semaphore system was only effective in good weather. The last semaphore signal was transmitted on 24 November,

1860, with morse code and the new system coming into use the following day.

Q

Quest for gold

To a young twelve-year old Anglesey boy in 1851, Liverpool was the door to the world. This was a fact of life, as there were few prospects open to him on his home island. Any child with a spark of ambition knew he had to leave home to carve a future for himself.

So it was that young William Williams, fourth son of Thomas and Elizabeth Williams, Pen y Parc, Pentraeth chose, like many of his contemporaries, to go to sea from Liverpool. He was quick to learn, and two years later was an able seaman on a sailing ship.

As did other boys, William heard of the fortunes men were making as they prospected for gold in Australia. Aflame with the spirit of adventure, he decided that that was the life for him, so he worked his passage, sailing on the 'Abah Bray' out of Liverpool, when he was eighteen years old.

The ship carried a large number of government emigrants among the seven hundred passengers and crew. In Australia William received a testimonial, two pounds of tobacco and '1/6 or 2/- on landing as payment for my work on the trip', he later wrote. The ship docked in Melbourne after one hundred and twelve days at sea.

William needed money for prospecting as he had to obtain a permit and take a stock of food and clothing, so he worked for eight months loading ships with ballast at nearby Williamstown. On a good day he could earn as much as £8, on average £24-£30 a month.

Word spread that gold was to be found at Canrona in Queensland, 'just picking it as one would pick potatoes or stones', so he determined the time had come to try his luck there.

A voyage of seven days took him from Melbourne to Rockhampton where, to his dismay, he found thousands of disappointed men waiting for ships to return to Melbourne. But William refused to be dissuaded, and joined three other prospectors. They spent three useless weeks searching before being reduced to penury, and having to beg for food. They did find a little gold finally, and could then leave the area having paid their debts but with little in their pockets to show for their efforts. He returned to Melbourne much the poorer.

Later, while writing his memoir of his early life, William reflected philosophically that he could have made a fortune and lost it in the hurricane when 'Royal Charter', the ship carrying more successful prospectors home to England, was lost off the coast of Anglesey.

He worked in Williamstown again for a time, to earn enough to buy clothing, then set off for the gold fields with three other Welshmen. Although they dug to a depth of one hundred feet there was little to be found. Persistence paid, however, when eventually, after three months, the four men made £300 each from their finds.

It was then reported that gold had been found in New Zealand. Intrepid as ever, William decided to see for himself. He sailed to New Zealand and prepared to make the long trek of a hundred miles over some hostile territory. His experiences were beyond his imagination – carrying a sixty-pound back pack across a range of mountains over eight thousand feet high in winter, sleeping rough or camping and almost, on one occasion, being washed away by a flooded river.

Rats, searching for food, plagued him and his companions at night. He and his group prospected during the hours of daylight, moving on as they worked but without much success. Eventually they fell in with another group of Welshmen and their finds increased until, collectively, they were able to finance and build huts for themselves and a chapel.

William then returned to Australia but went back to New Zealand later to join one of his brothers. They worked together over very difficult ground, finally achieving success on one site where they found gold to the value of £2000 to be shared among five.

Over a period of twelve years William Williams had struggled to make his fortune. He made one final attempt in New South Wales where, with only sixpence in his pocket, he borrowed ten shillings to open a new stretch of ground. His luck changed dramatically. In nine weeks he and a companion found gold to the value of £1100 each. He repaid the friend who had lent him ten shillings by giving him part of the ground.

This time, with money in his pocket again, William wisely decided enough was enough and planned to return home. On 14 December, 1871, he sailed on the 'True Briton' from Melbourne having collected messages from his fellow Welshmen who hailed from Anglesey and Caernarfon to pass on to their families. He banked his money safely with the Bank of New South Wales in Melbourne.

Before sailing, he had bought himself a harmonium, which he took on board for the voyage home and on which he played hymn tunes to while away a tedious journey. The passengers, himself included, took turns to cook for a week at a time. Some had brought food with them and were willing to share. It was a long, tiresome voyage as tempers frayed occasionally while living in cramped conditions.

The ship docked in early April 1872, and William Williams made his way back to Pentraeth, almost fifteen years after he had left. His first task was to visit old friends and deliver the messages to the families of those he had left behind in Australia.

Three years later he moved to Liverpool again. This time, if details on his marriage certificate are to be believed, he found work as a railway porter. Two years later a new career began. He used the money he had saved from his gold prospecting days and borrowed more to buy a plot of land on Parliament Fields where he built houses for rent. This was an astute move as the port was expanding rapidly and housing was desperately needed for workers who were attracted by the more substantial city wages.

William Williams's interest in religion remained with him throughout his life. He was particularly active in the development of Sunday Schools in Liverpool and worked tirelessly for the newly built Welsh Calvinistic Methodist chapel in Princes Road, where he was an elder. Like many prominent Liverpudlians of his day he was a keen Liberal.

As a boy, William Williams had received little education. When he first became a sailor his knowledge of English was sparse, but over the years he improved his linguistic skills until by the time he was ready to launch his new building career he was a fluent speaker and writer in both languages. He was a Victorian who overcame many difficulties, accepted many challenges, and ended his life a successful businessman. When he died in 1915 he was able to leave a fortune of thousands of pounds to his family.

R

Royal visitors – Georgian and Victorian

Throughout the 19th century the royal family visited Anglesey several times, either when passing through on their way to and from Ireland, or on longer visits when they were able to be tourists and holidaymakers.

Since the shortest sea crossing to Dublin was from Holyhead, this was the passage chosen by George IV in 1821. The occasion provided an excuse for the townspeople to demonstrate their loyalty. Preparations were under way well before the expected visit. The king would arrive by sea from the south before embarking for Ireland following a stay at Plas Newydd.

The *North Wales Gazette* reported the arrival of an advance party of twenty of the band of the 7th Hussars in the packet 'Meteor' from Dublin. They treated the town to two or three pieces of 'delightful music' before leaving in stage coaches for Plas Newydd where the king would be spending the night.

'These circumstances allowed us to expect that our revered King intends honouring old Anglesey with his presence in a few days, which we heartily hope he may and in no part of his dominions, we state it without the least hesitation, will His Most Gracious Majesty be received with more pure affection or where there is a debt of gratitude will be more strictly acknowledged,

103

than in his zealous and very loyal Principality of Wales,' wrote the Gazette reporter.

Readers of the newspaper were informed in advance of plans for the royal welcome:

When H. Majesty's yacht and the squadron in attendance are descried from Holyhead Mountain a single beacon or Fire will be lighted on the Mountain. One Fire on a Hill near Tre Iorwerth. One Fire on Bodafon Mountain. One Fire on Llwydiarth Mountain and one Fire on Dragon Hill. As soon as the Royal Squadron gets within Holyhead Bay two fires will be lighted on the above-named stations.

Should the arrival take place in the daytime dense columns of smoke will present themselves instead of Fires. On the landing of His Majesty the welcome tidings will, of course be announced by the discharge of cannons from Holyhead.

The king landed on August 7th, soon after four o'clock in the afternoon, to be met by the Marquess of Anglesey. A triumphal arch on the pier was festooned with laurel and flowers, surmounted by a regal crown supported by two Welsh harps. Baize-covered steps on the side of the jetty eased the royal landing and led to a temporary platform in front of the lighthouse on Salt Island where His Majesty met officials.

Following the official presentations, the royal party with the Marquess in attendance, left in 'three carriages and four' for Plas Newydd. They arrived between seven and eight o'clock to the sound of a royal salute from cannon on the lawn and from the 'Cheerful' revenue cutter anchored in the Strait below the house. The 7th Hussars band provided music. The route to Plas Newydd was lined with spectators. King George IV was left in no doubt about the warmth of the welcome. He stayed overnight after sitting down to dinner. The Gazette reported 'His Majesty did not appear to be in high spirits as the news of the Queen's illness had been previously conveyed to him.'

Her death on August 10th, was announced as the king prepared to set sail for Dublin from Holyhead. Bad weather, however, kept the royal yacht in harbour for a few days. Celebrations were curtailed on hearing of the Queen's death. George remained on board the yacht, and little was seen of him or reported on his state of mind – the rift between Queen Charlotte and himself was already common knowledge. He was finally forced to leave for Ireland in the steam packet boat (his first experience of sailing under steam) as this was deemed safer in bad weather. The royal yacht followed. The steam packet 'Lightning' was re-named 'Royal Sovereign' after the trip.

The cooking of the royal dinner was undertaken ashore, and the meal taken on board before the boat sailed. The king, his spirits now lifted, was said to have enjoyed his meal and complimented Captain Skinner, in charge of the packet, on the menu and quality of the food, and presented him with a set of engraved wine glasses as a token of his gratitude.

The next royal visit took place in August 1832 when the then Princess Victoria spent some time on the island as part of an acclimatisation exercise before her accession to the throne. It was decided that she should visit parts of Wales to familiarise herself with the Principality and its people.

After her crossing of the Menai Suspension bridge, which was but seven years old at the time, the guns of yachts moored off Craig y Don fired a royal salute as the procession made its way along the picturesque water side approach to Beaumaris. The royal standard was hoisted on the castle, and an elaborate welcome awaited the royal party at The Bulkeley Arms Hotel.

The Princess and her party walked across The Green, admiring the view across to the mountains, and boarded a barge from the royal yacht which was anchored nearby. They cruised around Ynys Seiriol (Puffin Island). On another day they visited Caernarfon. The Princess was impressed by Beaumaris and its environs.

Her stay at The Bulkeley Arms Hotel was curtailed when she and her party moved on to Plas Newydd, possibly because of an outbreak of cholera in Beaumaris. As a guest of the Marquess of Anglesey, Victoria was able to enjoy riding around the estate on her pony, 'Rosa'.

While out riding one morning she tore her habit. The nearest tailor who could be entrusted with the repair was a local lay preacher with the Methodists who lived nearby at Llanfairpwll. The dress was delivered to him on a Sunday morning but, royalty or not, he was adamant that he would not mend it until the following day as he had a preaching appointment elsewhere. Instead of not being amused at the delay, Princess Victoria admired the tailor for being loyal to his principles – an opinion which, no doubt, endeared her to the local Welsh chapel-goers.

By 1847 Victoria was Queen and had married Prince Albert. In August that year the royal party's summer break began when they sailed in the royal yacht up the Irish Sea to the west coast of Scotland, having embarked from the Isle of Wight where they had been in residence at Osborne.

Victoria wrote in her diary:

Having arrived at the entrance of the Menai Straits, we left the 'Victoria and Albert' and went aboard the 'Fairy', the 'Victoria & Albert' with the 'Black Eagle' (the two equerries having joined us), the 'Undine' and the 'Scourge' proceeded around the Isle of Anglesey by

Holyhead and, in the 'Fairy' accompanied by the 'Garland' we went into the Strait.

The weather was good, and she wrote of the splendid mountain views over on the Caernarfonshire side, and the lower Anglesey landscape.

We passed close to Plas Newydd where we had spent six weeks fifteen years ago. I felt as if I remembered it all very well but admired the scenery even more than I have expected from my previous recollection.

The 'Fairy' also passed the shore where the giant tubes were being assembled for Stephenson's Britannia Bridge, past the Swelly rocks, and under the Menai Suspension bridge. News of their approach had travelled swiftly. The Queen wrote: 'There were crowds of loyal people in steamers and boats, playing "God Save the Queen" and cheering tremendously'. She, Albert and her brother Charles landed and strolled over the suspension bridge. Later, on their return to the royal yacht, the Queen pronounced the visit to have been a great success.

The Britannia Bridge was completed in 1850. Stephenson's unique design had intrigued both Victoria and Albert, so they and four of their children paid a brief visit to inspect it closely. They travelled by horse and carriage from Bangor over the suspension bridge to Llanfairpwll station, to be met there by Stephenson himself, who had arranged for an engine and a coach to be there to take them to the bridge entrance on the Anglesey side. The Queen's carriage was hauled part way into one of the tubes by workmen, then the party was conducted to the shore to view the massive structure from below. Prince Albert and the young Prince of Wales had the unique experience of walking across the top of the tubes, accompanied by Stephenson.

On another occasion Victoria paid yet another visit to Plas Newydd when she, Prince Albert and the Duke of Cambridge and suite stayed on the island. They also visited Bodorgan Hall in the absence of the owner, Owen Meyrick, but were able to see the house, admire his pictures, and tour the gardens. The orchidaceous house pleased them, as it contained many of the rare species of air-plants recently introduced into Europe.

A royal visit to Ireland in 1853 proved to be another red-letter day for Holyhead, when J.H. Rendel, engineer in charge of the breakwater project then under construction, conducted the royal party around the harbour works and the quarry. They also visited South Stack.

Holyhead had yet another royal visit in 1859 when Prince Albert arrived during October to inspect 'The Great Eastern' which was anchored off-shore.

When the Harbour of Refuge at Holyhead was completed in 1873 the Prince of Wales and the Duke of Edinburgh travelled on the quarry railway to the end of the breakwater to open the new harbour officially.

As the century ended, Queen Victoria, then an old lady of over eighty years of age, travelled to Ireland for the last time. A diminutive figure in black, she spent ten minutes in Holyhead being transferred from train to boat in a wheelchair pushed by her Indian servant and accompanied by her ladies in waiting. Security was strict throughout her train journey across Anglesey. All crossing gates on the railway were locked and guarded by a plate layer with flags and detonators to hand, should the signals break down. Traffic was stopped on adjacent lines until the royal train had passed, and, as extra insurance, a pilot engine travelled a short distance ahead. Station staff lined the platforms at each station. It was doubtful whether Her Majesty was aware of all the precautions.

The 19th century had passed, and a new way of life was about to begin.

S

Schooldays gone by

When Anglesey head teachers began to log the activities at their schools little did they imagine the rich source of information they were setting down for posterity about a way of life on the island many years ago. A collection of these log books at the county record office in Llangefni is one of the island's treasures.

How different schooldays were at the end of the 19th century, for both children and staff.

In Llanfairpwll the first head teacher appointed to the Board School in 1871 received a salary of £70 a year, out of which he had to pay his pupil teacher £4 and the sewing mistress £4.10.0 a year. A year or two later the caretaker received £5 – £1 more than the pupil teacher.

The children attending school were expected to pay 1d a week as infants; 2d a week as children learning to write, and the older children in the top class paid 3d a week. The School Board supplied lesson books for children whose parents could not afford to pay for them. In 1884, slates which were used widely in Anglesey schools cost 4s 8d a dozen.

In 1885 the headmaster of Llanfairpwll left to take up work elsewhere and the newly appointed head had to provide 'ink, foolscap paper, books etc. and charge the children for the same. The Board will supply chalk to the amount of 2s 6d per year, and the following books – 2 dozen

Royal Primers, 2½ dozen Royal Readers, 1 modulator (for teaching Tonic Sol-fa), 1 Johnson map of Scotland.' At this time, the schoolmaster was given £1.10.0 towards coal for use in the school, but he could also ask parents for contributions towards heating the classroom.

School attendance in country districts was governed by the seasons. Absence increased when mushrooms and blackberries were to be picked, and when help was needed on the farms.

Local events often provided an excuse for absence from school . . . the old custom of 'clapping eggs keeping some away' and on 13th May, 1890: 'Llanfechell Spring Hiring Fair, gave half day holiday in the afternoon'.

Holidays were also given when the schoolroom was needed for other uses. Communal use of school premises is nothing new. On 4th October, 1886 the Llanfechell Log reads: 'This afternoon the school was closed, the room being required by the Dorcas Society for their annual distributing meeting'. On 22nd January, 1889: 'The school was closed, the Polling Booth for the County Council Election being held therein'. On another occasion: 'No school this afternoon on account of public meeting held in connection with the University College for North Wales'. And the occasion in 1892 likely to please the boys: 'Holiday. The Volunteers held their shooting competition in Cemaes'.

In 1895 school closed for half a day: 'The Lord Manor's Court being held at Cemaes in celebration of which the school children had a tea party.' Church events also took precedence over lessons: '23rd September 1884: Opening of Llanbadrig Church after its restoration, consequently no school today', and '29th June 1892: Closed school for remainder of week owing to the Association at Amlwch and tea party on Friday at Bethesda chapel'.

The different seasons also had their effect on attendance. One June record states: 'Hoeing turnips has spoiled our

111

average these days'.

Holyhead children were marshalled to carry water during a shortage: 'March 1897 – Owing to the water famine from which Holyhead is now suffering many children are kept at home to carry water', and again in October: 'Owing to the water famine necessitating the keeping of many of the children at home to carry it from distant wells, the attendance today is low and is likely to be so all week'.

Before the introduction of free education, the payment of school fees was a constant bone of contention. The Cemaes head teacher in 1889 recorded: '14th October: A boy, John Hughes, Top Street, was this morning sent home because he had no school fee. His mother came to school in a great fury and made use of very improper expressions adding that she would pay no more than a penny, the fee for the third standard being 2d.'

Illness and disease, such as the dreaded smallpox, diphtheria, influenza and typhoid, could close a school. In April 1882: 'Few children in school – the fear of diphtheria keeping others away. One child died from that disease yesterday.' A fortnight later: 'Another child of Cemaes died last week from diphtheria'.

In 1888 smallpox struck the village: '6th January: The week ending today cases of smallpox have been reported in the village. Parents are panic-struck.' A week later: '11th January: A fatal case of smallpox has happened. The coffin has been outside for two days there being no one that will venture to place the corpse in . . . four other cases are reported. We deemed it to be the wisest plan to close the school till the place is clear of the epidemic.'

In February 1898 the head teacher wrote: 'A great deal of illness and fevers such as diphtheria, typhoid and influenza are raging in the adjacent neighbourhood. Every precaution to avert their introduction to this district is attended to. Lime has been freely used around the school and offices, together with disinfectant, Condy's Fluid, inside. The children have been advised to wear a little camphor about their body'.

Keeping the smaller children warm in cold weather was important to this thoughtful Cemaes head teacher. In January 1892 he wrote: 'The children were dismissed this morning. Many have their backs very thinly clad and their feet not well protected and to retain them with wet feet and damp clothes would endanger their young lives to ruination.'

At Llanfaelog, school attendance was affected by work at home. On 28th June, 1889: 'Attendance this week is much below the average owing to several of the children being engaged in weeding and haymaking', and on 16th August: 'Broke up at noon for the harvest holidays'. But work was not the only excuse. In February 1891: 'A meeting of the Anglesey Harriers at Pencarnisiog affected attendances greatly one afternoon, and clapping for eggs also cut down numbers.'

On 14th September, however, the Llanfaelog head teacher recorded with some pride: 'School opened with unprecedented good attendance – no doubt it is the outcome of free education.'

A country school depended heavily upon the weather for good attendance: '23rd October, 1891: Exceedingly wet at school time this morning. Rhosneigr children are prevented from attending school on account of the impassable state of the road caused by the overflow from Maelog Lake.'

It was not only in country districts that the weather affected school work. In Holyhead one entry on a cold February day read: 'Very cold weather. During the cold weather it is deemed advisable to give the children as little slate and paper work as possible for the little ones' fingers are so benumbed with cold that it is almost cruel to give them writing work to do . . . Owing to the increased severity of the weather few children attended. These were dismissed at 10 a.m. and no school kept on Thursday.'

The weather had a spin-off effect in July 1881 when it was recorded that 'attendance very thin this morning and afternoon, the reports of two shipwrecks near Porthdafarch having probably tempted the children in that direction'. And in March 1886: 'The wreck of the S.S. Missouri near Porthdafarch yesterday morning is, in addition to the bad weather, an inducement to the elder boys to remain away from school this week.'

Visiting shows, local tea parties, preaching meetings where parents took their children, Sunday school outings, all part of the complex pattern of country village life, would take precedence over school.

As famous personalities passed through Holyhead to and from Ireland the children there were allowed to be bystanders and, no doubt, cheer and wave flags. In 1890 at Holyhead: 'The attendance in the afternoon is remarkably thin owing to a number of children having gone to the Mail Pier to see the Queen of Roumania passing through to Ireland.'

The weather did not only affect pupil attendance. Teachers could be caught unawares, too, as the entry for 16th October, 1891 at Holyhead records: 'The weather being extremely stormy the attendance is comparatively thin. Mr R. Pritchard (assistant) absent from duty this day. It appears that having gone aboard one of the ships in the harbour last evening he was unable owing to the state of the weather to get ashore in the morning and consequently had to remain aboard all day. He came ashore in the evening and apologised for his enforced absence.'

Dealing with miscreants in the 1890s was as problematic as it is today, albeit for different reasons. The Llanfaelog head teacher in April 1885 wrote: '25th April: I was compelled this morning to expel Percival A. Harrison for impertinence. He had the audacity to stand up in his place and say "I did not come to school to be knocked. My mother told me to tell her if I am knocked!" The power to punish being taken out of my hands I had no alternative in the interest of the discipline of the school but to expel the boy at once.'

The log books tell of the constant battle fought by teachers against poor facilities, the lack of suitable materials, and the disinterest on the part of some parents about the importance of education for their children. Anglesey was still, even at the turn of the 19th century, a place where the poorer families struggled to make ends meet, where children were expected to pull their weight at a very early age and where education was still regarded by some as a luxury.

T

Teetotal lapse

Today, when standards in society are more relaxed, it is easy to forget how strait-laced the Welsh chapels could be during Victorian times, when a member could be excommunicated for the slightest reason. What shame surrounded the solemn occasion as the act took place in front of the congregation.

Robert Roberts, one of ten children born at Mynydd-y-Gof outside Bodedern, whose father was an influential doctor, a farmer and a stalwart of Capel Mawr in the village, wrote reminiscences of his early days in Anglesey for his children, and had them printed for private circulation in 1905.

He described David Roberts, his father, as a dour character, a model of propriety, senior elder at his chapel and a strong opponent of the established church. He was a fervent teetotaller, supporting the movement against strong drink which was sweeping across Anglesey in the wake of nonconformity.

Dr Roberts was responsible for conducting the week-night society meeting at the chapel (Y Seiat), in the absence of a minister. It was he who had to deal with a reported fall from grace of one of the younger members, Iago Hughes.

Iago Hughes had been accused by another chapel member, Ebenezer Watkin, a local shopkeeper whom the villagers secretly believed to be cheating his customers by giving short weight although he was never charged openly.

He visited Dr Roberts to make his accusation. Robert tells the story:

Ebenezer Watkin came forward in a fawning way, apologising for giving trouble. My father waited till he opened the subject of his visit, which he presently did in a heart-broken sort of voice. 'It is a painful subject I am come about' . . . It was Evan's way to arouse expectation before getting to business. Then, putting on a look of distress, but alight in his eye betrayed a gleam of enjoyment . . . 'I am sorry to say that he got drunk at the fair and fought Wil Owen Crydd (cobbler) on the way home'. He seemed to dwell on the words as if he enjoyed repeating them. My father and mother were greatly surprised and shocked at the news.

Ebenezer Watkin, gaining confidence as he caught the undivided attention of his listeners, coloured his story by describing the two men as being 'covered in blood'. Was this matter sufficiently grave to be brought before the society? David Roberts believed it was.

When the society meeting was convened, there was an unusual number of members present. Some would have been shocked, others curious to see the outcome.

'My father and mother had a conversation whether it was proper that we young children should be present', wrote Robert, 'but my father held that discipline being an ordinance of the church – and a very solemn one – it was the duty and privilege of children to witness the administration of it for their edification. I am afraid we thought little of that view of the subject. But we were intensely curious to see Iago and to see how he would look under the ordeal, and especially how he would look

117

when turned out which we took for granted, from all we had heard, he would be.'

Robert had a child's dislike of society meetings, usually finding them boring. On this occasion he said:

The readings and prayers were longer and more tedious than ever, the singing more unutterably dreary and dismal. At length the preliminaries were over and my father got up. A pin could have been heard to drop. After a few coughs – coughs of importance were much in vogue with the Methodists, both deacons and preachers, at this period, and I don't think have quite disappeared to this day – the proceedings commenced.

Iago Hughes, it was reported, had sold a cow at the fair, and, as was the custom, turned into the local public house, the 'Crown' in Bodedern, with the buyer to settle and have a glass of ale. While in the 'Crown' Iago met Wil Owen Crydd and began to argue the merits of the established church of which the cobbler was a communicant. This was a time when feelings ran high between church and chapel. The argument became heated, no doubt fuelled by the consumption of liquor, and the two men turned to fisticuffs outside the premises to defend their principles.

Dr Roberts, in a few words, pointed out the enormity of the offence, the dangers, the increasing use and abuse of strong drink and 'the wiles of the evil one'. He called the miscreant to stand before him and asked what he had to say in answer to the charge. Robert records the conversation which followed:

'I don't attempt to deny the charge,' said Iago in what I thought a healthy tone of voice and then continued: 'But I wish to say that I only drank four glasses of ale, and they were small ones.'

Dr Roberts then produced the 'Cyffes Ffydd', the denominational rule book, and read out the rule relating to the so-called offence. He then put it to the vote, and the congregation elected unanimously for Iago Hughes's expulsion.

Then my father announced in his most serious manner that he was no longer a member of the church of Christ on earth. He then gave him an earnest exhortation to humiliation and repentance. The proceedings so far had been impressive and dignified. No one had spoken but my father and Iago. All eyes were now riveted on Iago Hughes.

Roberts, child as he was, had expected some visible change in Iago Hughes, but was astonished to see him:

. . . going coolly to his seat to fetch his hat and when he had found it from under the seat and come down to the bottom step, he there stopped and looked around and said 'Well, as you like. As I said, I don't deny the charge. But I only had four glasses'. This he said in a light manner. Then in an altered tone he added, 'There are worse than me here. There are some here that can take double the quantity and sit smoking and drinking for a whole afternoon in a public house'.

Continuing in the same voice but looking unmistakeably at Ebenezer Watkin, he said: 'And there are some here who are guilty of worse things than drinking a glass or two of ale'. This unexpected turning of the tables left a most uncomfortable feeling upon all present. I could not help looking at Ebenezer Watkin and thought I perceived a sort of shudder pass over him, but, of course, all that might have been fancy. At any rate, Iago did not look as he walked with a light step and opened the outer door and disappeared into the darkness.

Later, Robert recalled the incident, and with hindsight added his own comment:

I have often thought that discipline, to be conducted with dignity, should be administered by persons of blameless character, and if possible by those of a little better position than the bulk of the members. In this case it was so, and was followed by no ill effect. And the mysterious hints thrown out by Iago had perhaps cleared the air. As for Iago, the effect on him had been very salutary for he soon sought re-admission into the Church, which all were very glad to accede to him.

U

U-boat stories

The First World War saw many Anglesey men serving in the Royal and Merchant Navies, especially from Holyhead. Some never returned.

German submarines were active in the Irish Sea and in the Mediterranean and their attacks were responsible for the loss of lives and harrowing experiences of many.

One of the Irish ferries operated by the London & North Western Railway Company, 'Hibernia', was re-named 'Tara' after being requisitioned and re-fitted for patrol service during the early years of the war. The years 1914 and 1915 found her patrolling the northern entrance to the Irish Sea between Scotland and Ireland. Then she was ordered to sail to the Mediterranean as part of the North Egyptian coastal patrol.

Friday, 5th November, 1915, was a date to be etched on the minds of those who sailed in her, for this was the day when a German U-boat struck when 'Tara' was eight miles off the north African coast at Solum. It took only eight minutes for the ship to sink, meanwhile 93 of the crew crowded in to the boats, to be taken in tow by the submarine and landed at Port Suliman as British prisoners of war. There they were put in the custody of the Turks.

This was inhospitable country. The crew were treated badly, being forced to march barefoot across rough terrain, sleeping in caves. There were casualties, but no offer of medical treatment except that which fellow crew members could provide. The body of 'Tara's' cook was buried on shore, his grave covered with stones against possible marauding wolves or wild dogs. There was no medical attention for the ship's carpenter who had suffered a fractured leg. He was forced to march with the rest of the crew so it was not surprising that he developed septicaemia.

There were no anaesthetics to hand and a Turkish doctor later had to amputate his leg without. One of the crew who kept a diary wrote: 'He did this with a sharp stone and blunt scissors'. The carpenter died. Paymaster Alfred Dutton of Holyhead, in his diary, commented: 'Very touching service was held by Captain Tanner, nearly everyone crying . . . most pathetic scene . . . everyone feeling very lonely and quiet.'

The men remained in the desert for several weeks, their condition deteriorating every day. Food was scarce, even snails were boiled to supplement their meagre diet.

On the forty-second day of captivity Dutton recorded:

Breakfast at 7.30, hard boiled rice. Having had a little more flour issued to us in lieu of shortness of rice, I managed to knead some flour and boiled rice together and wrapped some in a leg of a Mahomed trouser and boiled it in a bucket. This proved a great success, nice and plump. It was divided into nine pieces and each with a big chunk in his hand and some tea in glasses, had a fine dinner. We promised another one for ourselves at Christmas.

Christmas 1915 came and went. Meanwhile conditions became desperate and even their guards faced starvation.

Three sheep are killed, all inside parts of two are being taken away, also two heads, by the guards. Firewood party all feeling really done up. Can hardly walk – on our knees taking the wood, no energy left to pull up some by the roots. Dinner and tea, boiled rice. Today looks very serious and very little hopes. Myself I don't feel like walking four yards but struggle on. Managed to gather more wood and more green vegetation and garlic. Dinner, boiled mutton and soup. Feeling done up. Must go for a good sleep. All officers and men are breaking down, some fainting in heat.

However, relief came unexpectedly, when a convoy of British motor vehicles including ambulances found them. It must have been a dream come true. The 'Tara' survivors spent some weeks in hospital at Alexandra before returning to a heroes' welcome in their home town of Holyhead.

The second tragedy occurred nearer to home, only days before the end of the war in 1918. The 'Leinster' was an Irish mailboat, sailing out of Kingstown (Dun Laoghaire) for Holyhead on 10th October with 757 passengers and crew; many of the passengers were soldiers on leave.

The ship was torpedoed by a German U-boat shortly after leaving the shelter of Kingstown harbour and sank in a few minutes. There were 193 survivors. One of these was Anne Carlisle, newly married at Rathgar in Ireland, who told her story to a national newspaper on the twentieth anniversary of the sinking. A copy of her story can be read at Holyhead Maritime Museum, alongside a model of 'Leinster' and a torpedo badge, one of several awarded to crew who were rescued. Twenty-three crew members lost their lives. There is a poignant mention of one, an engineer, who had changed places with a colleague as a favour on that voyage.

Anna Carlisle's account of the tragedy is riveting. She describes how she remained on deck while her husband went below, and of the obvious anxiety on the faces of her fellow passengers as they looked out to sea where hidden danger lurked. This was to have been the start of her honeymoon. Without warning the torpedo struck a shivering blow to the bow of the ship. It did not explode but penetrated the postal office where mail was being sorted. Twenty sorters were drowned immediately. Separated from her husband Anna Carlisle was hustled into a lifeboat. He caught sight of her and jumped in beside her at the last minute before the second torpedo hit the heart of the vessel, splitting her and blowing everything into the air – machinery, boilers, chairs and tables, trunks, and mutilated bodies. In two minutes 'Leinster' disappeared beneath the waves.

Rescue came an hour later, with a destroyer steaming to their aid, but not before the lifeboat was almost filled with water from high seas and the passengers bailing out to little effect with hats, shoes, any receptacle which would hold water. The lifeboat was dashed against the steel side of the destroyer and upturned, throwing Anna and the passengers into the sea. Then, mercifully, it righted itself and she and her husband managed to clamber aboard. Ropes hauled them aboard the destroyer, which returned them to Kingstown.

Anna and her husband had lost nearly all their possessions, but retained the most prized possession of all – their lives.

The Irish Sea had many such stories to tell during two world wars.

V

Visitors to the Menai Strait

The 19th century saw an influx of visitors to Anglesey.

As the 18th century ended and the 19th began the Rev. William Bingley who styled himself 'Fellow of the Linnean Society and later of Peterhouse, Cambridge' set out on his tour of Wales, writing down his experiences as he went. He began his journey into Anglesey from Caernarfon, using the Tal-y-Foel ferry. His first impressions were not favourable:

'The interior of the island appeared to me to be very ill attended to,' he commented when referring to cultivation, 'and in addition much of the land lies in peat bogs or is full of low rocks which cannot be cleared but by blasting, and that at enormous expence (sic) . . . The general face of the country is low, flat, and unpleasant and although it has been represented as nearly covered with wood in the time of the Druids, there is now scarcely any other than what is found in the plantations on the south east coast.'

Bingley visited Llanddwyn, turned his back on Anglesey and, on a glorious day, appreciated the view of the mountains, which appeared to placate him somewhat. But the possibilities for smuggling around Llanddwyn did interest him. He wrote:

This place, I have been informed, is a noted resort of smugglers and their traces are indeed sufficiently evident on several large and deep holes dug in the sand for concealing the cargoes. I have seen few places more inviting to this species of illicit commerce. Several narrow entrances between the rocks with a fine sandy bottom seem particularly calculated to hide their little vessels from the careless eye of the revenue officers of this district. Here they can run in and (being four or five miles distant from any inhabited place and surrounded by eminences) unload and deliver their cargoes to their emissaries without apprehension.

Bingley stayed in Caernarfon and one morning joined the cutter belonging to the hotel: 'a beautiful little decked vessel with accommodation for ten or twelve persons and her pilot', to sail to Ynys Seiriol (Puffin Island).

Although the weather was fine and the prospect of a sail enticing, the actuality was far from uneventful. All went well until they had passed Plas Newydd.

Not far from hence are the well known rocks, called from the numerous currents that set in different directions around them, the Swelly Rocks. We had a wind directly across and in one of our tacks, though I had but just been talking with the pilot on the subject and every possible precaution was used, the bow of our vessel caught one of the eddies and, in spite of every effort, bore us directly on the rocks.

I seized the helm and my companion who was stronger than myself sprang with a boathook to the bow of the vessel and before she could touch the rock so strong was the surrounding current he pulled her off. A different current bore us furiously against the tide, which now caught our bow and bringing us again around, with considerable violence near the deep of the channel, the vessel righted and we had the good fortune the second time entirely to clear these.

He added:

> The circumstances altogether threw us into some little tremor for the swelling and violent bubbling of the water in some places, the rapid and furious tideway through the deeps, the roaring of the water in consequence of the submarine rocks and the dashing of the foam and spray in the various whirlpools and against the rocks that are exposed with the roar and turbulence around are, at some particular times of the tide, of such nature as scarcely to be described.

The Swelly Rocks now carry a marker and a light, but still pose problems to unwary sailors.

The church of Saint Tysilio on its tiny island intrigues him, but, obviously not knowing the story of Anglesey's many saintly connections, he was critical of its position:

> What should induce the foundation of a church in so singular and precarious a situation where the service can only be performed when the tide serves, I am not able even to guess. I fear, when a small wind blowing in the course of the tide during the service, sets it in sooner than had been expected, as must sometimes happen, the sensations of the congregation are not of the most pleasant nature imagineable. The struggle to escape before they were hemmed in by the tide would be too ridiculous to be compatible with the sacred duties of public worship and it is much to be lamented that there should be any necessity for it.

William Bingley's experiences on Ynys Seiriol are among the very few recorded by visitors to this part of northern Wales during the period in which he wrote. Having negotiated the perils of the Swellies, the cutter sailed without further incident towards Beaumaris and the island, where he hoped to see birds and wild life.

> I happened here to be carelessly leaning over the side of the vessel when I observed vast quantities of a species of medusae, Sea-blubber, float past. By means of a small net I got out two or three specimens . . . when handled they are found to blister and when fishermen find them in their nets are very careful not to touch them with any exposed part of their body but generally kick them out with their shoe.

He intended to observe seabirds on Ynys Seiriol, puffins in particular, and was not disappointed, thanks to the initiative of the pilot who fired a swivel gun:

> . . . to try the effect of the report around the island, when such a scream of puffins, gulls, and other sea birds was heard as beyond all conception astonished me. The immense multitudes that in a moment rose into the air were unparalleled by anything I had before seen.

There was another treat in store for this perceptive traveller:

> We landed, and I clambered up the rocks and walked along to the other side of the island, when I had a sight that even surpassed the former . . . upwards of fifty acres of land were literally covered with puffins. I speak much within compass when I declare that the number here

must have been upwards of 50,000. I walked gently towards them and found them either so tame or so stupid as to suffer me to approach near enough to have knocked one or two of them down with a stick. I laughed to see them tumble over when running to take flight, by their bills catching on little eminences that they were not aware of.

The young are pickeld (sic) for sale by the renters of the island and form an article of traffic peculiar to this neighbourhood.

Time, and the ravages of an increased rat population, have decimated the puffins on Ynys Seiriol. Two hundred years after William Bingley visited, one is fortunate to see these comical and colourful inhabitants.

Harriet Alderson was the daughter of a Rotherham ironmaster who married into a wealthy family, her husband being Rector of Aston near Sheffield. They were close friends of the Fitzherbert family of Tissington Hall, Derbyshire, who joined them on their visit to northern Wales in 1818. Three carriages were necessary to take both families, their servants and their luggage. The long trip began at Aston in September when they made their way to Tissington then across Cheshire and by Denbigh, St Asaph, Abergele, Conwy to Abergwyngregyn where we take up Harriet's account:

Soon we came to Aber where there is a ferry to Anglsey and from which place Beaumaris appears to great advantage – with feelings of the greatest pleasure we anticipated our residence for six weeks in so picturesque a spot.

Telford's Suspension bridge was yet to be built, so travellers to Anglesey chose either this ferry crossing, or the Bangor ferry which was more popular because it was shorter and not so fraught with danger. Harriet's party chose this one.

We proceeded to Bangor Ferry two miles distant where there is an excellent inn with boats and every accommodation for conveying passengers across to Anglesey. After remaining here a short time we became impatient to reach the place of our destination and everything being combined to render the scene as imposing as we could wish. The sky was cloudless.It was high water and the sea particularly clear and transparent. The views each way here were delightful. We were quickly ferried over and after a charming drive of five miles on an excellent road made by Lord Bulkeley amongst rock and underwood, we reached Beaumaris with the most favourable impressions.

Their caravan of coaches created a stir, as she recorded:

We have a large party and were in three carriages, the number was apparently a novelty to the simple islanders as they crowded around us to see us alight. We found the Inn and were made comfortable and received every attention from the landlord.

Harriet does not give the name of the inn, but she continued: 'We remained at the Inn till we were suited with lodgings which were obtained without difficulty and at an astonishingly cheap raite.'

Harriet was pleased with her visit to Beaumaris, commenting frequently on its beautiful position and the amenities for visitors:

Baron Hill, the seat of Lord Bulkeley, is close to the town. His grounds are open to all who wish to enjoy a quiet walk. The evening views from many parts of these walks are particularly grand. This castle was also one of Edward I's. It is remarkable for its low towers. The only thing wanting to tender Beaumaris perfect is sand. The shore is shingly which also tenders the bathing very unpleasant.

Harriet quotes the French saying, 'Ainsi point de roses sans épignes' – no roses without thorns – but continues:

There are no bathing machines but Lord Bulkeley has built a bathing house on a part of the shore and where bathing women always attend. A warm sea bath belonging to Lady Bulkeley may be made use of by applying to the people who live at the principal lodge. No place affords a greater variety of interesting walks combined with the finest inns imaginable. Service is performed at the church three times every Sunday, twice in Welsh and once in English . . . the duty throughout is admirably performed.

Some years later Augusta Pearson visited Beaumaris. She was a vivacious young lady, mature in her outlook and not afraid of speaking her mind. Augusta was born in Mitcham, Surrey. Little is known of her family, but she travelled with 'Charles and Cara' and kept her diary, dedicated, as she put it, 'without permission to my Three beloved sisters'. The title she gave it explained the purpose of the trip – 'A Spinster's Tour through North Wales in search of the picturesque and sentimental'.

Augusta, Charles and Cara sailed from Liverpool to Beaumaris, a popular way of travelling to northern Wales during the 19th century. her first impressions of the town were of 'a cheerful, pretty looking place'. Like many, tourists to the increasingly popular resort they stayed at The Bulkeley Arms Hotel.

Augusta proclaimed The Bulkeley Arms Hotel to be:

A most comfortable one and they can moreover boast of a very good cook and very civil servants. Our room with a bow window overlooks the sea, and the pier, which is paid by subscription, two pence for everybody.

She was quick to notice 'a vast assemblage of idle men and boys who add considerably to the picturesque, lounging over the wall'.

As do so many visitors to Beaumaris today, Augusta chose to make the trip to Penmon: 'a pretty secluded spot' where she admired the Priory church and commented: 'Those monks were very knowing old Gentlemen and evidently knew what was good in every way'. This visit is remembered in a previous chapter of this book, 'Meeting the People'.

Augusta was impressed when she saw the Menai Suspension bridge for the first time:

A most stupendous affair it is. I was hardly cognizant of its immense size till we saw a carriage on the bridge which looked more like a spider on a large beam than anything else. The iron work looks very light and graceful but the piers are rather heavy and ugly.

She continued to be impressed when, on another day, she sailed through the Strait from Caernarfon:

We were fully impressed with the enormous height of

the bridge and the immense span thereof. When under it I don't know that I ever felt so insignificant before.

A trip to see Stephenson's recently opened Britannia bridge was planned, too, but the tide did not allow them to go by boat so they walked along the shore 'until we reached the wondrous thing'. They were fortunate as 'a train came rolling through as we stood beneath it and the sounds were something terrific. We were invited to walk through the tube and a guide was at hand to conduct us, but neither Cara nor I relished the idea,' she admitted.

At each end there are two enormous stone lions which cost 500£ a piece. It seemed to me the 2000£ might have been spent to more advantage but no doubt I am wrong.

The grey mansion of Plas Llanfair below the bridge did not impress her. It was later to house the 'Indefatigable' training school, and today is a Ministry of Defence outdoor pursuits centre:

We saw Clarence Paget's house facing the river and just above the bridge. It did not look particularly pretty but I dare say they have a nice view of the opposite coast from their windows.

Today's visitors to the Strait may sit on the terrace at Plas Newydd and watch small craft from the Plas Llanfair centre and the Plas Menai Watersports Centre at Felinheli pass to and fro. They may even make a trip themselves – a cruise from the dock at Plas Newydd which would surely have interested William Bingley, Harriet Alderson and Augusta Pearson had it been available in their day.

W

Who says Anglesey is flat?

Nobody who has travelled across Anglesey will refute the claim made by those who know, that the island is hilly. 'Undulating' might be more correct, with several more abrupt outcrops which Anglesey people proudly call 'mountains'. Nothing over 220 metres high, but mountain nevertheless.

These higher lands saw the earliest habitation on the island. Evidence of substantial hut circles and forts still exist, now quiet, heather-clad, the haunt of birds and wild life. Their sites have been searched by archaeologists who have discovered a way of life unique to these upland areas.

Anglesey boasts six mountains – Mynydd y Twr (Holyhead), Mynydd y Garn (Llanfair-yng-Nghornwy), Mynydd Parys (Amlwch), Mynydd Eilian (Llaneilian), Mynydd Bodafon (Penrhosllugwy) and Mynydd Llwydiarth (Pentraeth).

Mynydd y Twr and Mynydd Parys are those most frequently visited, the first for its important collection of hut circles and fort, and the hair-raising approach to the visitor centre at South Stack; the second for its copper mining history.

All five command wide views of the island. On a fine day, when atmospheric conditions are right, the Isle of Man can be glimpsed on the horizon.

Mynydd y Twr rises behind Holyhead, a bastion on the

very edge of the Irish Sea, looking down on the town and the sheer cliffs of the North and South Stacks. This part of Holy Island, although only a couple of miles from urban Holyhead, has its own distinctive atmosphere. The village of Llaingoch and other tiny communities at the foot of Mynydd y Twr have housed smallholders and quarry workers and farm labourers, hardy folk who have contributed to that atmosphere.

Men have settled on Holy Island since early times, no doubt attracted to the area as being a safe lookout for marauders who might attempt invasion from the sea. 'Cytiau'r Gwyddelod' is a collection of remains of around twenty huts dating from the second to the fourth centuries. Farther up the mountain are the remains of an early fort, probably positioned there to overlook the Irish Sea and to offer an early warning system.

Today's visitors flock to Mynydd y Twr to see these and to visit South Stack lighthouse, and Ellin's Tower perched on the cliffs opposite. Comparatively few make their way to the summit to look around at the seventeen-acre site of the Iron Age fort which archaeologists believe must have been a refuge, a strong point where settlers from lower down the mountain could go in time of danger. There is no evidence of a date of occupation, but the experts believe Caer y Twr (the fort) is an Iron Age foundation but could have been used by the Romans later. They think a Roman warning beacon could have occupied the summit where the Ordnance Survey marker now stands.

Below the summit, above the North Stack, 19th century communications designers built the first of the series of eleven telegraph stations between Anglesey and Liverpool, where messages were received and transmitted by semaphore to and from ships rounding Anglesey, to the ship owners and merchants in Liverpool – see the chapter 'Passing the Message'. A fog signal was placed at the tip of

North Stack, very necessary in an area regarded by masters of the sailing ships as one of the most dangerous around the coast of the British Isles.

One slope of Mynydd y Twr was defaced in the 19th century when it was quarried for the substantial amount of stone needed to build the long breakwater which encloses the New Harbour at Holyhead. This provided work for many living in the scattered communities, as had the building of the lighthouse on South Stack some years before. Today the quarry area is a country park, the heathery slopes and summit of Mynydd y Twr a vantage point favoured by visitors, and Ellin's Tower a mecca for those who study bird life on the cliffs through the binoculars of the RSPB whose centre it now is.

Across Holyhead Bay, standing sentinel over the north-western tip of Anglesey, stands the 170 metres high Mynydd y Garn. From its windswept summit views extend over the rugged and remote corner of the island at Carmel Head to the Skerries lighthouse off-shore, westwards to Holyhead and Mynydd y Twr, and south and east across a less-frequented countryside of small farms and hamlets towards the centre of Anglesey. Down below, closer to the coast, lies the late 17th century house of 'Mynachdy', associated over a number of years with the family who had control of the Skerries lighthouse before they sold it to Trinity House for £444,984 during the 1800s, and as the one-time home of an Anglesey doctor who befriended a shipwrecked boy who grew to be famous for his gift of bone-setting.

To Llanfair-yng-Nghornwy, whose church tower can be seen below, came the Rev. James Williams as rector. He built himself an imposing rectory, lobbied incessantly for a lifeboat service for Anglesey, and was instrumental himself in helping to save lives from shipwrecks off this dangerous coast where so many ships foundered in the days of sail.

The summit of Mynydd y Garn and land on its slopes are

now administered by the National Trust. Several paths from the surrounding lanes lead up to the marker on the summit.

Mynydd Bodafon (178 metres) is accessible from Penrhosllugwy or Maenaddwyn. Bronze Age implements have been found here, yet more evidence of early habitation of an upland site. A short scramble to the summit of Mynydd Bodafon from the lane at the foot rewards the visitor with a bird's eye view of the whole of Anglesey against a background of the northern Wales coast as far as the Great Orme and the mountains of Snowdonia. There are scattered ruins of cairns, hut circles and terraces still to be found on the mountain if one knows where to look among the heather and bracken. Down below the summit the lane passes along the side of a rush-fringed tarn which gives the impression that this could once have been a volcanic area.

When George IV passed through Anglesey on his way from Ireland, a chain of bonfires was lit to announce his arrival at Holyhead. One of these was lit on Mynydd Bodafon.

Mention has already been made of the remote atmosphere of the Mynydd y Twr area at Holyhead. The same can be said of the tarn around which houses and cottages are clustered here at Mynydd Bodafon. In the days before the invention of the motor car, existence in remote places such as this must have been lonely in the extreme, and the communities self-contained.

Remains of the old works buildings on the top of Mynydd Parys above Amlwch are a well known sight to every visitor to this part of Anglesey.

Copper ore has been mined intermittently on Mynydd Parys since very early times. The 18th century and into the 19th, saw the greatest activity, when the need for copper to bottom ships of the Royal Navy boosted the industry and the copper mines of Mynydd Parys became the most extensive in the world.

Today some research continues to find other minerals for which the mountain is reputed to be particularly rich, but the old workings are silent. This is a moonscape. Abandoned shafts are dangerous places. There are stagnant pools, copper coloured. A ruined windmill is all that is left of the only five-sailed windmill in Wales at one time.

Although the site is forbidding to the unwary, a locally formed Trust has plotted a safe trail around the mountain where visitors can appreciate some of the mining methods of the day, the dangers experienced by the miners, and the sudden development of the little town and port of Amlwch in the wake of industrialisation.

At one time copper coins of the realm were in short supply, so the Parys mines provided copper for provincial tokens which were put into circulation. Over 250 tons of Anglesey pennies and halfpennies were minted in a little over ten years.

Information boards in the car park on the Llannerch-y-medd to Amlwch road, close to the summit, tell the story of the mountain. At the Sail Loft above Porth Amlwch there is a more detailed exhibition which tells the story in full.

Mynydd Eilian (177 metres) south of Point Lynas, is scattered on its lower flank with housing, but marked by a group of telecommunications masts below the summit.

A few miles down the eastern side of Anglesey lies Mynydd Llwydiarth (158 metres). This overlooks the small village of Pentraeth. At one time the sea reached the village (the name means 'the head of the strand') and one flank of the mountain fell steeply into the water. Hidden in the afforestation now covering most of Mynydd Llwydiarth are two Bronze Age cairns. There are also remains of a hill fort, smaller than but similar to that on Cae'r Twr, Holyhead. This stands on a naturally precipitous site of about an acre, and could only be approached from one side.

Anglesey's 'mountains' may not be of sufficient challenge

to warrant climbing gear, but their various attributes and long history make up for that deficiency.

X

X marks the spot

Memorials and commemorative plaques abound in Anglesey and refer to local people who have made their mark, or events too important to be forgotten.

Shipwrecks around the island were commonplace at one time, and none received more publicity than that of the 'Royal Charter', lost in a hurricane off the coast near Moelfre in October 1859. A large iron steam clipper carrying bullion worth £300,000 and 390 passengers, many of them bringing with them the fortunes they had made during the Australian gold rush, she was on her way home to Liverpool. It was a night of unprecedented storm. The ship hit rocks, no rescue was possible, and nearly all on board perished. The memorial on the cliff above the site of the wreck is simple, but poignant.

A shipwreck on the west coast is recorded on a small stone opposite the sea-girt rock, Maen Piscar, off Holy Island. A Liverpool-bound ketch struck the rock on a dark, foggy night in September 1819 and immediately began to sink. As she did so the captain's dog, Tyger, jumped into the sea and struck out for land. His master, two sailors and a boy followed, trusting the dog's instinct to lead them to the shore. Tyger's instinct was unerring. They reached land, exhausted. Tyger licked the captain's hand, and died. The memorial stone on the coastal path between Rhoscolyn and Trearddur reminds walkers of Tyger's bravery.

There are also plaques on schools and public buildings to commemorate worthies who were educated there or lived locally.

The tiny hamlet of Llansadwrn, above Beaumaris, displays one of these on the wall of the old primary school, recalling Thomas Williams, born on a local farm in 1737, who became one of Britain's most famous industrialists in later life. He was articled to a solicitor in Denbigh then returned to Anglesey to be assistant to a Beaumaris lawyer. Later he was appointed steward to Lord Boston who had estates on the island. Thomas Williams leased Llanidan Hall from Lord Boston, and undertook work for other wealthy landowners as his reputation grew.

Copper was found at Mynydd Parys, Amlwch. Thomas Williams arranged legalities for the Lewis family of Llys Dulas on whose land the copper had been found. He became involved in the business and, in 1778, joined with others to create the Mona Mine Company and the Parys Mine Company which were soon two of the greatest industrial projects of the 19th century. His business acumen made Thomas Williams wealthy. He was generous, giving money to local causes, and he farmed successfully. His influence was more widely felt in that he was MP for Great Malvern for some years. When he died in Bath in 1802 Thomas Williams owned several mansions and left a fortune of half a million pounds. He is buried in Llandegfan churchyard.

Visitors who flock to the tourist attractions of Llanfairpwll could fail to notice the plaque in the wall of 'Tŷ Coch', the large red brick house opposite the War Memorial. This house was the home of Sir John Morris Jones, an Anglesey boy who grew to be one of Wales' finest Welsh language scholars.

John Morris Jones was born at Llandrygarn, a few miles away, but the family moved to Llanfairpwll when his father opened a shop there. John began his education in the village, continuing at Friar's School, Bangor, and Christ's College, Brecon, from where he won a scholarship to Jesus College, Oxford. In 1889 he returned to Wales as lecturer in Welsh at the University College in Bangor where, six years later, he was appointed professor. John Morris Jones's great contribution to Wales was his Welsh Grammar which at the time filled a dire need. He was knighted in 1918. He died in 1929 and is buried in St Mary's churchyard overlooking the Menai Strait.

Travellers on the Amlwch road between Llugwy and Penysarn comment on the tall stone column standing high in a field above. This was erected to commemorate the lives of a famous local family of four brothers whose home was at Pentre-eiriannell nearby. They are known in Anglesey as the Morris Brothers – Lewis, Richard, William and John – all talented in various ways and compulsive letter-writers.

John, the youngest, is the least well known. Like many of his contemporaries he went to sea as a boy. He died off the coast of Spain while serving on a man-o-war, when only twenty-eight years old. Richard left Anglesey to seek his fortune in London when he was fifteen. After living in poverty for some time his luck turned and he secured a post at the Admiralty where he rose to be chief clerk for foreign accounts to the Comptroller of the Navy. Like his two older brothers, he was more cultured than John. He collected literary manuscripts and later oversaw the publishing of bibles at the SPCK. In 1771 he published his edition of the Book of Common Prayer in a large illustrated format. Richard is especially remembered in Wales for being the founder of the Cymmrodorion Society of which he was President until he died in 1779. The Society is still active today.

The brothers wrote many letters – 1000 in all – William, the second son, wrote 400, 300 of them to his brother Richard.

William lived in Holyhead where he worked as Comptroller of Customs. He, too, collected manuscripts. He was a knowledgeable botanist and a keen gardener. He loved church music and was choirmaster at St Cybi's church.

Lewis, the oldest brother, is the most famous of the four. In 1729 he was appointed Inspector of Customs for Beaumaris and Holyhead on a part-time basis, a post he held until 1743. While in Anglesey he was commissioned to survey some of the Welsh ports. He produced charts of the coast of Wales from Llandudno to Milford Haven and an atlas, 'Plans of Harbours, Bars, Bays and Road in St George's Channel', which included twenty-five detailed plans of Ynys Seiriol and Black Point, Traeth Coch (Red Wharf Bay), Dulas beach, Cemlyn, Holyhead, Malltraeth, Llanddwyn and Abermenai which were published in 1748.

In the 1740s Lewis was appointed under-steward for Crown lands and moved to Cardiganshire. He died at Goginan, his second wife's home, in 1765 and is buried at Llanbadarn Fawr, Aberystwyth.

Anglesey witnessed a unique early aviation experiment. On the beach at Llanddona there is a plaque which commemorates the event and the man responsible for it. This is where W.E. Williams built and flew an aeroplane in 1913. He was a physicist who, after researching in Glasgow and Munich, returned to his University College at Bangor to lecture in physics. His dream was to build his own aircraft, and he was helped to realise this by two local industrialists, one providing finance, the other allowing him to use a plot of land to build a temporary hangar. The plaque records his test flight in September 1913 when his 'Bamboo Bird' flew at a height of seven feet at thirty-seven miles per hour. It must have been a great occasion for the residents in this quiet corner of Anglesey.

These are but a few of Anglesey's memorials, which are

numerous and varied, from simple gravestones in country churchyards to the more ostentatious like The Anglesey Column which greets the visitor passing over the Britannia bridge to the island. This commemorates the bravery of Henry Paget, later 1st Marquess of Anglesey, on the battlefield of Waterloo.

Ynys Môn County Council has an on-going scheme of providing plaques to the memory of those who have brought fame to the island in various walks of life.

Y

Yoicks! Tally-ho!

The tradition of throwing hot pennies to the crowd from the balcony of the Bulkeley Hotel, Beaumaris, has a special place in Anglesey's social history, and is closely related to the story of the Anglesey Hunt.

The Anglesey Hunting Club, as it was known, was formed in 1757 with Beaumaris as its meeting place. A pack of hounds was lodged at Baron Hill nearby. The Club attracted subscribers from the county élite of the island – Lucinda Bayly of Plas Newydd was its first Lady Patroness. The two leading figures of Comptroller and Lady Patroness had to prove some connection with the county families of Anglesey, Caernarfon, Denbigh, Merioneth or Flint, or be descendant of past Comptrollers.

The Hunt meeting took place in November, with the annual Ball, a glittering occasion for Anglesey, held near Christmas at Beaumaris Town Hall. The first subscription to the Club was five shillings. There were twenty-five members.

On the occasions when there was a dearth of foxes on the island, it is said that a fox was 'imported' from the mainland, housed in a shed overnight before being released for the chase the following day. Hares were also hunted, or a drag organised, and there is even a record of a carted stag being used.

The Anglesey Hunt became very popular as the years

passed. Newspaper reports tell of sixty men and women riding at a meet at Plas Gwyn, Pentraeth, in 1882, and before another meet over one hundred enjoyed a hunt breakfast.

As with many organisations, those in charge complained that not all members were punctilious with their subscription payments. In some cases the minutes showed they were reprimanded or even threatened with further action. During the late 1700s, for example, an army Major had neither paid his fee nor his hotel bill over the period of the hunt. The secretary advised him if no money was forthcoming the Colonel of his regiment would be informed – a threat which doubtless had the required effect.

Each officer had his or her duties to perform. The Comptroller headed the team. The Lady Patroness, chosen because she was 'young and beautiful', had to contact the headmaster of Beaumaris Grammar School to arrange for the boys to be given leave of absence to attend the ceremony of hot coppers which was part of the Club's activity in aid of the poor. Coppers would be heated to a high temperature then the Lady Patroness would shovel them out of a container and toss them over the heads of the assembled crowd, when gloved hands would scramble for them.

The Anglesey Hunt Club was regarded as something of a marriage bureau, where like met like and often a wedding would be the result. Ellen Williams of Bodelwyddan, Lady Patroness in 1832, met her future husband, William Owen Stanley of Penrhos who was Deputy Comptroller that year, in this way.

Dress was considered important, especially among the officials of the Club, who wore badges of office. Originally the men's dress was a blue frock coat with scarlet velvet collar, a scarlet cloth waistcoat trimmed with silver, and white breeches. The Lady Patroness wore a red silk sash with a gold or silver Druid's head on the shoulder and at the hip a miniature gilt hunting horn on two small chains.

In its heyday the Anglesey Hunt ran no fewer than five packs of hounds, and records tell that they were fed on oatmeal, barley and sheeps' trotters.

The Ball at Beaumaris Town Hall at the end of the season attracted the élite to the little town, where all was bustle at the various hotels and in the Town Hall. Music was provided for dancing by fiddlers, harpists, and even French horn players. It was an occasion for uniforms and ball gowns, the dancing being led by the Comptroller and his Lady Patroness. No doubt the townspeople would have gathered to watch arrivals, and to listen to the music through open windows.

Another spectacle for the townspeople was the procession after a morning's hunting, when the meet made its way to the Bulkeley Hotel for refreshment. They assembled at Turret Lodge on the Baron Hill estate, horses and riders and any followers in their own conveyances, to make their way down Church Street, past the castle and the court house on to the edge of the Green, back to Castle Street and the hotel entrance. A band played. The streets would be packed with onlookers. Bands included those of the Royal Welch Fusiliers, Royal Marines, the 'Clio' training ship moored in the Strait off Bangor, and local bands.

During the late 1800s the Bones Supper became a feature of the last Hunt week of the season. It was a time for the younger members to relax and enjoy themselves in some horseplay of a different kind. After the ladies had retired for the night the men would tour the hotels and the streets of Beaumaris, forming rival bands who would chase each other noisily, lay booby traps, and keep the neighbourhood awake by banging pots and pans and blowing hunting horns. They tied room doors together at the hotel, which caused consternation the following morning as the occupants attempted to emerge for breakfast. Today, such behaviour would be regarded as a breach of the peace. In the 1880s

Beaumaris accepted it with good humour, high spirits being regarded as part of the Hunt tradition.

In the early days Hunt traditions were jealously guarded. Anyone proposing to do away with 'the customs or any other of the ancient usages be fined a Pipe of Port Wine'.

Times have changed, and the Anglesey Hunt has changed with them. Today around twenty subscribers, mostly from Anglesey, maintain the meets which occur from the end of September every Saturday until the end of January, as a drag hunt.

Latterly the Ball has been held at Henllys Hall, but because of the conversion of the property to apartments the Hall is no longer available, and the 2005 event, held on the first Friday in February, was at the Celtic Royal Hotel in Caernarfon, the nearest venue to Anglesey which could accommodate the number of subscribers and their guests.

One colourful remnant of the old days of the Hunt remains for all to see. This is a Hunt scrapbook written by Gwenddolen Massey of Cornelyn Manor, Llangoed, now in the Bangor University archives. Gwenddolen was one of the two Massey sisters whose botanical studies are a valuable treasure at Oriel Ynys Môn.

She wrote the scrapbook in easily legible hand. The book is prefaced with a large photograph of her sister Edith, dressed in green riding habit, a bowler with a face veil and a bunch of violets below her stock pin. She stands by her horse. Gwenddolen recorded all the local hunts in her scrapbook, which is a work of art as well as a valuable record. Animals and flowers tumble down the margins in a riot. Foxes and rabbits are all drawn in gold, and they have red glass eyes which gleam as one turns the pages.

The Anglesey Hunt is a vibrant part of the island's social history.

Z

Zealous clergymen

Anglesey has been known for its charismatic preachers, especially since the surge of nonconformity which swept the island during the late 18th, the 19th and the early 20th centuries. But even in the days before the religious revivals, when it was common for many of the clergymen of the established church to sit back in their parishes and take life easily, the occasional firebrand let his voice be heard as he preached against the laxity of some of his parishioners.

The Rev. Thomas Ellis at St Cybi's church in Holyhead was a man with strong convictions. He was not an Anglesey man, having been born in Flintshire and educated at Jesus College, Oxford. In 1737 the College offered him a 'lectureship' at St Cybi's which led to his becoming rector, and he served the town well for a number of years. Thomas Ellis is remembered for sweeping away old traditions which he believed sinned against the teachings of the church, but had been maintained for centuries.

To Thomas Ellis, the way in which patronal festivals were celebrated was anathema. What had once had great religious significance was getting out of hand. He chastised his parishioners from the pulpit and decided it was time for action.

In a society which was hard-working, with little time for pleasure, patronal festivals were eagerly anticipated as an opportunity for enjoyment of the baser kind. Holidays they may have been, but certainly not holy days any longer.

William Morris, the Holyhead customs officer and a friend of Thomas Ellis, wrote to his brother Richard in London, explaining that on three Sundays in July the relics of St Cybi were on view, so these patronal occasions had acquired the name Relic Sundays. They had become the excuse for feasting, drinking, fighting and swearing and were enjoyed by the townspeople as well as those who came in from the country districts for a day's relaxation.

Thomas Ellis would have none of this. He was a fiery, puritanical preacher who made his opinions known fearlessly. He instigated a moral clean up which incensed some, but made him many friends among the more serious-minded. The sanctity of the Sabbath was important, so he persuaded the youth of Holyhead to hold their local celebration on one day only – July 25th – which was a weekday and with a more diluted form of entertainment. Instead of the atrocious behaviour of the past there would be organised competitions, running races and dancing, with silk handkerchiefs as prizes. To a populace who rarely possessed such a luxury the prospect of owning and sporting a silk handkerchief was enough to make them forget their previous unseemly behaviour.

Like his fellow clergy in the established church, Thomas Ellis condemned Methodism. He did, however, support the formation of the circulating schools which appeared in the wake of nonconformity. His enthusiasm for educating the children of the town became a reality when he opened a school in the little chapel alongside St Cybi's church, which carries a plaque to that effect today. His efforts in education were marked years later when one of the Holyhead schools chose to bear his name.

Baptists throughout Wales knew of the powerful oratory of the Rev. Christmas Evans. Born in 1766 at Esgairwen, Llandysul in Ceredigion, he began his working life labouring on the farms around his home. At one of these he came under the influence of a farmer who also ran a school, where young Christmas learned to read Welsh, English and a little Latin.

When he was twenty-one years old he joined the Baptist church and became immersed in the revivalist movement, to the extent that he undertook joining a mission to south-west Caernarfonshire.

Christmas Evans used drama to great effect in the pulpit, a popular ploy appreciated by chapelgoers who had tired of the staid, featureless preaching in the pulpits of the established church. They were ready for the fire which Christmas Evans could provide. So the one-time farm labourer became a full-time preacher. In 1789 he was ordained.

By then the Baptist message had reached Anglesey. Chapels had been built at Cildwrn (Llangefni) and Mynydd Parys (near Amlwch). Other groups met for services in private houses. There had been some ill-feeling between groups of Baptists at one time, but they were reconciled again, and, as a body on the island, invited Christmas Evans to minister both churches and all the groups.

His strong, dramatic preaching led to an increase in the congregation. He was held in high esteem wherever he went. In fact, such was his popularity that this egotistical preacher began to adopt an attitude which proclaimed to all: 'I am the Bishop of Anglesey'. Other denominations regarded the Baptists wryly, and referred to their ministers as 'Christmas's chickens'.

Christmas Evans' oratory, his commanding personality and voice stood him in good stead, and he was in demand all over Wales to fill pulpits on special occasions. But his growing dictatorial attitude began to rile some of his Anglesey congregations and slowly his popularity on the island waned.

When his wife died, he became a lonely figure. He left Anglesey after some years and undertook ministries in southern Wales in 1826, in Caerffili and Cardiff, and later, in Caernarfon. Christmas Evans died in Swansea while on a preaching tour in 1838.

The period of this powerful preacher's responsibilities in Anglesey coincided in part with the dominance of the Rev. John Elias over the Anglesey churches of the Calvinistic Methodists. He was another gifted orator.

John Elias was the son of a Caernarfonshire weaver, eight years younger than Christmas Evans, and was ordained into the Calvinistic Methodist church in 1811. He married and went to live in Llanfechell where his wife kept a shop. They had a short married life of seven years, before Elizabeth Ellis was lost at sea while returning home to Anglesey from Liverpool. Two years later John married again, this time the widow of Sir John Bulkeley of Presaeddfed, and the couple went to live in Llangefni.

John Elias, like Thomas Ellis before him, was fearless in his condemnation of many social practices which, in his opinion, denigrated gospel teachings. He condemned drinking, swearing and all forms of gambling. His congregations were subjected to tirades of criticism, and his pointed finger in personal accusation became his trademark. The custom of gathering jetsam after shipwreck was an activity he abhorred. This, in his book, was no less than stealing.

John Elias died in 1841 of gangrene of the foot. His funeral on Anglesey was an occasion for general mourning, as shops closed, blinds were drawn and people lined the streets to watch the cortège pass. There is a plaque to his memory on the wall of the Moriah CM chapel in Llangefni.

The large CM chapel in the middle of Brynsiencyn will always be associated with the Rev. John Williams who was minister there for a time. He began his ministry in 1876, moving to Liverpool in 1895 to take charge of one of the large Welsh congregations in the city. When he retired from full time ministry in 1905 he returned to Brynsiencyn. During the First World War he was deeply involved in recruiting men for the Forces and was made an honorary captain for his efforts. His constant pressure on young men to fight for their country was not popular with some, who believed that a minister of religion should show no preference one way or another.

The age of oratory in the pulpit seems to have disappeared. Today, congregations appreciate briefer, more pithy sermons with fewer histrionics. How Thomas Ellis, Christmas Evans, John Elias and John Williams would have disagreed!

Further reading

Royal Commission on Ancient Monuments: Anglesey

Gwynedd Archives Service: The Menai Bridges

T. Telford, 1838: The Life of Thomas Telford

Robert Stephenson: Chester & Holyhead Railway Reports

Miriam Griffith, Magma Books: Chester to Holyhead, Travelling the Old Post Road

Anglesey Antiquarian Society & Field Club Transactions

Dewi Roberts, Gwasg Carreg Gwalch: An Anglesey Anthology

C.G. Harper: The Holyhead Road – The Mail Coach to Dublin

Ed. Parry: Royal Visits and Progresses to Wales

Queen Victoria: Leaves from the Journal, Our Life in the Highlands

E.A. Williams: Hanes Môn yn y Bedwaredd Ganrif ar Bymtheg

Dewi Roberts, Gwasg Carreg Gwalch: Visitors Delight

Quartermaine, Trinder & Turner, CBA Research Report, Council for British Archaeology: Thomas Telford's Holyhead Road

John Ripley: The Britannia Bridge 1845-1850

Edward Pugh: Cambria Depicta

Augusta Pearson: A Spinster's Tour through North Wales

G.J. Freeman: Sketches in Wales

William Cathrall: Wanderings in North Wales

Charles Dickens: An Uncommercial Traveller

William Bingley: North Wales, Vol. 2

George Borrow: Wild Wales

Thomas Pennant: Tours in Wales

Harriet Alderson: Diary of a visit to Wales

Edwin Roland Owen: Mynydd Twr

Frances Lynch, A.A.S.: Prehistoric Anglesey

Nancy Mitford: The Stanleys of Alderley

Capt. G. Butterworth: The Story of Penrhos

D. Lloyd Hughes and Dorothy Williams: Holyhead, the Story of a Port

Ann & Mary Jones: Diary

Skrine: Tours 1798

Helen Ramage, A.A.S.: Portraits of an Island

Y Bywgraffiadur Cymreig